Travel Fast or Smart?

PERSPECTIVES

Series editor: Diane Coyle

Travel Fast or Smart?

A Manifesto for an Intelligent
Transport Policy

David Metz

LONDON PUBLISHING PARTNERSHIP

Published by London Publishing Partnership
www.londonpublishingpartnership.co.uk

Published in association with
Enlightenment Economics
www.enlightenmenteconomics.com

ISBN: 978-1-907994-59-3 (pbk)

A catalogue record for this book is
available from the British Library

This book has been composed in Candara

Copy-edited and typeset by
T&T Productions Ltd, London
www.tandtproductions.com

This book is dedicated to
Ben, Hazel and Louis

Contents

Preface

Britain does not have a coherent transport policy. And conventional transport economics has reached a dead end.

This book sets out the principles that could underpin a strategic policy for transport. Instead of focusing piecemeal on getting from place to place ever faster, we need to think about how and where we want the economy to develop, and about how new digital technologies can help achieve this development.

We each spend about an hour a day, on average, on the move. This mean travel time has not changed for many centuries. Improvements in the transport system and technologies enabling higher speeds have sent us further rather than reducing travel time, so horizons have vastly expanded, both for individuals and for society.

We are now at a point of transition. Individuals in developed economies like the UK are no longer travelling further, so in future growth in the total amount travelled will be slower, driven mainly by population increase. At the same time, new digital technologies will clearly be important in managing the efficiency of journeys, but the potentially large impact of this technology is uncertain.

A transport policy should incorporate systematic thinking about the travel needs of society and the means by which those needs can best be met. However, in Britain, public investment in the transport system has been extraordinarily volatile. We closed underused railways and then experienced a doubling of passenger numbers that has prompted huge new investment. We gave up making substantial investment in motorways, but have now chosen to revive the road construction effort in a big way. We vacillate on road pricing, introducing congestion charging successfully in London but backing off because of local opposition elsewhere. We have delayed for decades the decision about whether and where to build additional airport capacity. The environmental impacts of transport infrastructure – both globally and locally – were once a key focus, but now are not.

This policy volatility is not wholly the consequence of the politics of left versus right. Rail was privatized but pragmatism, not politics, brought part of the system back into the public sector. An earlier Conservative government also privatized and deregulated buses outside London, hoping for benefits from on-road competition that largely failed to materialize. The present Conservative government therefore intends to allow other cities to opt for the successful London approach, in which the public transport network is well integrated under political oversight.

It is particularly striking that the current Conservative government plans a major increase in public expenditure on the transport system despite financial austerity. Senior politicians are keen on big investments in transport infrastructure, particularly in the north of England and in London, and in big projects such as High Speed 2 (HS2) and a third runway at Heathrow airport. Many of these plans are controversial, generally on account of their environmental impact. But there are also questions about who benefits and who loses, and about 'opportunity costs': how public money might otherwise be spent.

In this book I argue that this mess has come about because policy has focused on big construction projects and time saving, instead of on the part people and places play in economic development. Transport moves people and goods through space. Investment that increases speed or capacity encourages more movement. The capacity gets filled, but no time is saved. New roads therefore rarely ease congestion.

The endless disappointment is due to the misleading techniques used for economic appraisal and for modelling supposed future benefits. Most of the models used by transport economists fail to consider the main consequence of transport investment: economic development as land is made more accessible. Conventional transport economics plays into the hands of those who want to invest in road construction – big civil engineering projects that involve shifting earth, pouring concrete, rolling tarmac.

Instead, we need to invest less in roads between cities and more in commuter rail, to foster economically dynamic cities and to ease pressures in the housing market. We should shift investment from costly road building projects to far more cost-effective digital technologies that will allow better and more intelligent use of the structures we have now. This is the basis for an intelligent transport policy for the twenty-first century.

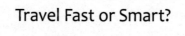

Travel Fast or Smart?

Chapter 1

An hour a day

The fundamental characteristic of travel behaviour – that on average we travel for about an hour a day – has important implications for any investment in the transport system.

To think about the future we need to look back at the past, both to see where we have come from and to judge what might be changing. How we travel in Britain has been tracked for the past forty years by means of the National Travel Survey. This is a large survey of households, commissioned annually by the Department for Transport. Individuals complete travel diaries covering seven days in which they record all the trips they make (excluding international air travel, which is considered in chapter 5). This survey largely reflects our daily travel, and it is world-leading in its coverage, detail and duration, to the great credit of the Department for Transport. It underpins much policy analysis.

Figure 1 shows how three key characteristics of daily travel have changed since the early 1970s. On average,

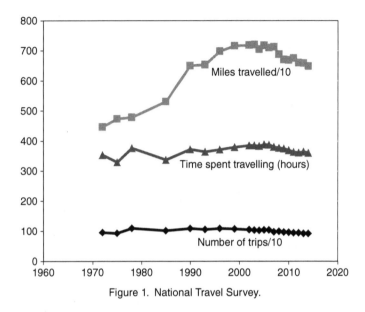

Figure 1. National Travel Survey.

people have made about a thousand journeys a year throughout the period. Of course, this is an average across the population. Some of us can rarely get out of the house, while others are hyperactive. Our travel patterns can vary considerably across our lifetimes. But the population average is useful for thinking about what is happening generally. In the case of the number of trips made, the stability over time is noteworthy.

The time we allow ourselves for travel has also been pretty stable, at about 360 hours a year, or an hour a day, as shown in the figure. This hour or so a day is found generally for settled human populations – a universal human characteristic. There are only twenty-four hours in the day and many activities that we must fit in: working, sleeping, eating, etc. This limits the time available for travel. On the other hand, there are many activities outside the home that require us to travel. There are also benefits inherent to travelling, quite apart from what we find at our destination. These benefits – the satisfactions from getting out of the house, stretching the legs, engaging with our surroundings, seeing the world – are experienced most intensely in leisure trips but are also present in daily travel. The balance between the attractions and requirements of travel and of all other daily activities yields the hour a day of average travel time.

The big change in behaviour over the past forty years has been the average distance we travel, which increased from 4,500 miles a year in the early 1970s to reach 7,000 miles by the mid 1990s, as the figure shows. Clearly, if we travelled further in the same hour a day, it was because we travelled faster. This was the result of investment in the transport system: private investment in more and better cars, public investment in roads, as well as investment in railways. The main increase in distance travelled arose from the growth of car ownership, prompted by the convenience of door-to-door travel where road space permits.

The figure also shows that there has been no increase in average distance travelled since about 1995. Indeed, there has been a small decline, probably in part due to the economic recession that started in 2007–8. So on a per capita basis, we have a stable, no-growth situation that has lasted for twenty years. This travel is mainly daily travel – the travel involved in going about our daily activities.

In subsequent chapters I am going to argue that this stability of daily travel will most likely continue into the future and should form the basis for transport planning. The implication is that future growth in the demand for travel will be driven by population growth and not by income growth, as was dominant in the past, when increasing personal incomes led to the growth of car ownership.

To understand the future scale and pattern of travel demand and how these needs might best be met, I must first discuss two key questions.

- Why have we chosen to take the benefits of investment in the transport system by travelling further (which is the subject of chapter 2)?

- Why did the growth in personal travel cease twenty years ago (the subject of chapter 3)?

But before looking at these recent developments, I want to track back in time, to see where we have come from. If we were able to follow the three lines in figure 1 back over two centuries, what would we find? The available evidence suggests that the average time spent travelling and the average number of trips have remained unchanged, but the distance travelled would have been about 1,000 miles per person in 1830. Why is 1830 the key date, and what is the significance of 1,000 miles?

One of the great technology breakthroughs of all time occurred in 1830: the opening of the very first passenger railway in the world, between Liverpool and Manchester. Before this, nearly all travel was on foot. Horse-drawn carriages on poor roads were not much faster than walking, and few could benefit. So the average speed of travel was walking pace – about three miles an hour. For an hour a day of travel, this would amount to about 1,000 miles a year on average.

The railway breakthrough depended on harnessing the energy of fossil fuel – coal, initially – to travel faster than walking speed. The nineteenth century was the great age of the railways, which offered station-to-station travel according to a timetable. The twentieth century was the era of the motorcar, which exploited the energy of oil to allow door-to-door travel at the time of your choice. The car is now responsible for three-quarters of the total distance travelled in Britain by all surface modes.

One reason the growth in personal travel has ceased is that we have run out of technologies that would allow us to go faster. We cannot travel faster on the roads – or not safely and with acceptable vehicle emissions. On the railways, we have high-speed rail on the way (discussed in chapter 6), but rail is used for a minority of all trips, and high-speed rail will be responsible for a minority of that minority, so little overall impact is to be expected.

The shift seen in figure 1 – from growth of average distance travelled to no-growth around 1995 – marked a transition between two eras of travel. Looking back, we can, in fact, discern four eras of human travel.

The first era began when our ancestors migrated out of Africa 60,000 years ago to populate the whole of the habitable Earth on foot. They were hunter-gathers who foraged for food, spending three or four hours a day on the move, as we can infer from the surviving hunter-gatherer societies. Individuals would cover some 3,000–4,000 miles per year.

Lifestyles changed, beginning around 10,000 years ago, with the cultivation of plants and the domestication of animals in settled communities. These early farmers worked hard because they could secure increasing returns from their efforts, in contrast to the foragers, whose extra efforts would deplete local resources and who would then need to move on to new territory. The farmers grew grain that could be stored and transported, which allowed the development of cities. Evidence of the size of historic settlements is consistent with an average travel time of an hour a day, reflecting both less need to travel in settled communities and more time required for productive work. So in this second era of travel, people covered about 1,000 miles a year on foot, largely going about their daily tasks and rarely venturing beyond the village or town where they lived. This era persisted until the coming of the railways.

The third era of travel, between 1830 and the 1990s in Britain, saw the exploitation of fossil fuel energy to travel faster and further, from 1,000 to 7,000 miles a year on average, and from a walking pace of three miles per hour to an average of twenty miles per hour. And now we are in the fourth era, when per capita growth has ceased and is unlikely to resume.

Chapter 2

Space not time

Since average travel time does not change, improvements to the transport system that allow faster travel result in us travelling further, which in turn results in increased access to land that can then be developed to support economic growth. This has important implications for the benefits we get from new investment and is the main focus of this chapter.

The findings of the National Travel Survey outlined in the previous chapter demonstrate that we have taken advantage of improvements to the transport system that allow higher speeds to travel to more distant destinations in an unchanged amount of time. What we might have done, but did not do, was to continue to travel to our previous destinations, thereby saving time in order to engage in other activities. Why is this?

We also know from the National Travel Survey that our reasons for travelling have changed little over the years. So why have we chosen to travel further for the same purposes? The answer is: to have more opportunities and choices. By travelling faster on the journey to work, we have a wider choice of jobs accessible from where we live in the time we allow ourselves for the commute, and more choice of homes that are accessible from our workplaces. Likewise, faster travel allows us a wider choice of shops, schools, leisure opportunities and so forth.

Suppose that you live in a village that is poorly served by public transport and that you do not have use of a car. Your opportunities and choices are quite limited. This is how some people in Britain, and many people in developing countries, live today, and how most of the people in the world lived 200 years ago. Modern transport has transformed both individual lives and whole societies by expanding horizons.

Transport serves to move people and goods through space. Investment in the transport system extends that movement. Travelling further by faster means of conveyance changes the geography of the country, which is how we see the impact of transport investments.

A good example of how transport investment can change urban geography is seen in London's Docklands. London was once the largest port in Britain, but the introduction of containers for general cargo using much larger ships rendered the city's docks obsolete. It took time to develop this large area of 'brownfield' land, in part because the area historically had poor transport connections. A key investment was the construction of the first phase of the Docklands Light Railway (DLR), a link to the City of London. This remarkably inexpensive development took advantage of disused railway infrastructure and derelict land for much of its length.

The DLR effected a step change in the accessibility of Canary Wharf, the nearest large vacant site, which made it evident to far-sighted developers that there was an opportunity to construct high-value accommodation to compete with the high rents in the City. There followed the parallel development of high-rise, high-quality office space and additional rail links: expansion of the DLR, an extension to the Jubilee Line, and refurbishment of old surface-rail routes to form the Overground. One hundred thousand people are now employed at Canary Wharf, and that number may double after the completion of Crossrail, a new underground line that is due to open in 2018. Beyond Canary Wharf, there are extensive residential and commercial developments, generally lower rise and lower value.

Public investment in the rail system made land accessible for development in Docklands. Private-sector developers then built commercial and residential property that serves to accommodate London's growth – both economic growth and population growth, employment and residential. This is the 'strategic narrative' that provides the context for individual investments. It is also the causal mechanism by which transport investment contributes to economic development. What we see, in economic terms, is that tenants at Canary Wharf are willing to pay high rents for the benefit of that location – rents that reflect the economic value added by these businesses, engaged in financial and related services. Such rents serve to reimburse the developers for the cost of construction and operation of the premises, and to offer a suitable return to investors. And these rents also reflect the easy access to Canary Wharf from central London, made possible by the new railways.

What we see in Docklands is not a new phenomenon. In 1840 the US was populated largely along the coasts and inland waterways, and it had an economy about the same size as Italy's. There followed a boom in railway construction that opened the interior to farming, mining and industry, and to new towns and cities. By 1890 the country had the largest economy in the world.

Transport economics

Oddly, transport economists don't appreciate this kind of explanation, which relates land use and value, and associated economic development, to transport investment. They suppose that the main economic benefit of such investment takes the form of time savings, which are valued because they allow more productive work to be carried out or more leisure to be enjoyed. (There are other recognized benefits, such as fewer road traffic casualties and reduced vehicle operating costs, that are not contentious and are therefore not considered further here.)

To value the time savings from an investment that adds an extra lane to a congested motorway, it is necessary to estimate the time savings per vehicle, the number of vehicles using the road, and the value of time saved to the users of the road. All three factors are problematic.

The value of time saved is estimated by asking a sample of road users how they would trade time against money. They are asked to say which they prefer from a number of choices of journey time and associated cost. This allows a conclusion about how much they are willing to pay to save time.

A transport improvement that allows faster travel will typically result in an increase in the numbers travelling – people for whom the destination was previously too far in terms of time taken. The convention is to value the time savings of the additional travellers as one half of the time savings gained by the original travellers (known as the 'rule of a half', based on textbook microeconomics). However, for wholly new rail routes such as those in Docklands, all travellers are new and so this halving applies generally, emphasizing the notional nature of time savings.

The more general difficulty with this 'travel time savings' approach to measuring the economic benefit of a transport investment that results in faster travel is that there is no evidence for any time savings in the findings of the National Travel Survey. Recall from the previous chapter that average travel time has remained at one hour per day for the past forty years, over which period there has been extensive public investment in transport infrastructure, with each scheme being justified on the basis that the value of the time saved outweighs the construction costs (after discounting, in the standard cost–benefit calculation).

So what has happened to all these estimated time savings? The answer is that the National Travel Survey findings in figure 1 show the long-run position. Time savings from faster travel are largely notional; to the extent they are real, they are short run. They are converted to increased distance travelled as people change their travel patterns, most importantly when they switch jobs or move house. People take advantage of faster travel to seek more choices and opportunities.

The approach of transport economists has been adopted by transport authorities generally, not least by the Department for Transport in the UK. In consequence, the case for investment in long-lived transport infrastructure is based on the value of short-run time savings. This is not a good idea in principle, and in practice is misleading about the real economic benefits of investment, as I shall explain. Moreover, transport economists disregard changes in land use, in part because they are difficult to predict within the standard framework and in part because including the increased land

and property values that result from improved access is seen as double counting benefits that have already been counted in the time savings.

The transport economists would like to believe that the initial time savings that supposedly benefit users of the improved system are efficiently converted to a whole variety of other benefits, including to land owners if rents rise as a result of improved access. If all the markets involved in this transmission are perfectly efficient, the value of the time savings would equal the value of the benefits as finally distributed. There are, however, two serious problems, which arise from the very tenuous linkage between the short-run time savings to individuals and the long-run changes to land use, as seen for instance in Docklands.

First, in practice, markets are far from perfect, and it is difficult to correct for imperfections, although some effort to do so is made (by estimating the value of what are known as 'wider impacts').

Second, time savings measure the totality of the benefits but give no indication of where or to whom the gains arise – the spatial consequences. The proposed new rail route High Speed 2 (HS2) will trim thirty minutes from the journey time between London and Birmingham. Such time savings are the basis of the economic case for the £50 billion investment, but this analysis does not predict the distribution of economic benefits between London and the cities of the Midlands and the North.

The political objective of HS2 is to boost the economies of these cities, but the conventional economic analysis is silent on distribution.

While rail investment can effect a step change in connectivity and access, the consequences of road investments are generally incremental. Nevertheless, the spatial distribution of benefits is also important for decisions on such investments, where the UK government plans to spend £15 billion over the next five years on the Strategic Road Network (the motorways and main trunk roads). This network is managed by Highways England (previously known as the Highways Agency), a company owned and funded by the Department for Transport.

Traffic congestion largely occurs near to populated areas, where local users take advantage of the network for daily travel, whereas away from such areas the traffic generally flows freely. About half the traffic on the M25 is long-distance users – those travelling between the south coast ports and the Midlands and the North, for instance, who want to avoid London, the purpose for which this orbital route was built. The other half is local traffic, particularly journeys to and from work, giving rise to the familiar morning and evening peak congestion periods.

The transport economists' approach to investment appraisal sees a congested motorway as an opportunity for investment to increase capacity. Time savings per vehicle multiplied by the large number of vehicles, and then multiplied by standard monetary values of time savings, generate total economic benefits that are compared with the construction costs to allow judgment about value for money. The time savings per vehicle are quite small, however.

Evaluation by Highways England of a large number of what it terms 'major schemes' indicates average time savings of three minutes at times of peak usage, less at other times. There is debate about the significance of such small time savings. On the one hand, it is argued that these are too small to change behaviour and so should be disregarded. On the other, it is contended that small time savings add up and so, logically, must be counted.

While small time savings on a long-distance trip are insignificant in behavioural terms, they are likely to be meaningful for a local user. The faster travel made possible by an extra lane or improved junction, for instance, opens up more opportunities and choices, particularly when people come to change jobs or move house.

In particular, in those many parts of the country where demand for housing exceeds supply, it must be expected that local users will take advantage of additional road capacity to seek more distant housing opportunities that they can afford. A similar effect is seen with urban rail improvements such as London's Overground. Some of the largest percentage increases in house prices in London in recent years have been found near stations on this route south of Docklands, in locations like New Cross, of limited inherent attraction but with relatively low-priced housing.

When analysing the case for road investments, it is important to consider the spatial implications: where different kinds of road user are located, and how they may benefit from the investment. For any commercial investment, it is of course routine to conduct a market analysis, asking which market segments will benefit. This is done for rail investments, where data from ticket purchases provides extensive information on users: allowing commuters to be distinguished from long-distance travellers, for instance. But for road investment, little effort is made to collect the data, particularly distance travelled and journey purpose, which would enable prediction of who would benefit.

Why we cannot build our way out of congestion

Available evidence is consistent with the proposition that most of the benefits of investment in the Strategic Road Network accrue to local users who are enabled to travel further on their daily trips. The extra traffic thereby generated is known as 'induced traffic', which is a consequence of road construction and arises because in the long run people take the benefit of faster travel by travelling further, not by saving time. This extra traffic means that congestion returns to its level before the investment was made, and long-distance traffic is therefore no better off. This is the basis for the maxim 'you can't build your way out of congestion', which we know from experience to be generally true.

At one time, ministers would quote this maxim – this was when they did not have a big road construction budget. Prime Minister Tony Blair, in his introduction to a 2004 transport white paper called 'The Future of Transport', wrote:

> We recognise that we cannot simply build our way out of the problems we face. It would be environmentally irresponsible – and would not work.

Nowadays, transport minsters tend to speak rather vaguely about new road schemes 'creating opportunities for hard-working people across the nation and driving economic growth' (as Roads Minister Andrew Jones said in September 2015), while no doubt hoping that congestion will be lessened, as is seemingly implied by the time-saving rationale.

In fact, the increased local access made possible by investment in additional road capacity leads to changes in land use: property development where planning consent is granted, increasing values of existing property where it is not. Such development is largely unintended. There is, however, a case for intentional road construction to foster development, but this needs to be led by developers and planners. If they agree that a site is suitable and commercially attractive for development, whether residential or commercial, and if investment in road access is needed to permit development, that could be an appropriate claim on a roads budget, whether local or national, subject to a value-for-money test.

An example is the plan for a new 'garden city' on a former military site at Bicester in Oxfordshire, where 13,000 new homes are to be built and where the Department for Transport has allocated £44 million for road construction, including a link to the M40. This illustrates both that new housing on such sites will require road investment on account of car ownership by residents, and that decisions about the location of such investment must be based on the intentions of the planners and developers: bottom-up planning, not part of a top-down national strategy.

The problem with congestion

While road investment can make land accessible for development, the rationale for most such investment is to relieve congestion. One stated aim of the British government's current Road Investment Strategy is a 'free-flow core network, with mile a minute speeds increasingly typical'. But if we cannot build our way out of congestion through investment in civil engineering technologies, how is this aim to be achieved?

One approach is to address the reason why congestion is a problem. Surveys of road users indicate that the most pressing concern is generally the lack of reliability and the uncertainty over journey time. This anxiety can be tackled by providing users with good predictive trip time information. An example is the motorway roadside variable message sign that predicts the time it will take to reach the next junction (although this is of course short range, and hence of limited utility). A more ambitious service is provided for freeway users in the Seattle area of the US, who can enter into the city's traffic website the locations of their home and workplace and the time they wish to arrive at work and are then advised the time to leave home to be at work on time nineteen times out of twenty. A further example is *Google Now* on mobile phones, which includes predictive travel times on the road system.

A rather different kind of predictive information that helps people cope better with traffic congestion is the time until the next bus arrives, as shown on electronic bus stop indicators in London and through many apps for mobile phones. Urban traffic congestion means that timetables cannot be relied on. The electronic indicators show the progress of buses in real time, allowing choices to be made accordingly and lessening anxiety about when one's bus might turn up.

As well as providing useful information to individuals that lessen unreliability associated with congestion, there are benefits to the road network as a whole. There are two kinds of road user: those who need to be at their destination at a particular time (e.g. those travelling to work or a meeting, or those making time-critical deliveries), who can use predictive journey time information to decide when to set off on their journeys; and those who are more flexible in trip timing (e.g. those who are going shopping or making morning/afternoon deliveries), who can use such information to avoid peak traffic. This is win–win: the more flexible users avoid peak times, the less the congestion experienced by those who cannot avoid them.

There is therefore a good case for a road operator such as Highways England to provide predictive travel time information to users in order to maximize network efficiency. The case for investment in such digital technology depends on valuing journey time reliability and also on the behavioural response of road users to such information, both of which can be established through research.

One reason for being hopeful about the benefits of predictive journey time information is the good experience of 'just-in-time delivery' in the road freight sector. Efficient road haulage businesses contract with their customers to deliver goods to a very tight time specification. For instance, a haulier may contract with a supermarket chain to deliver from a central warehouse to individual stores within thirty-minute time slots, or pay a penalty – the haulier can achieve this by taking advantage of real-time information about the position of each vehicle and traffic conditions. A senior executive of a major road freight business once told me that unanticipated traffic congestion was less of a problem for performance than unanticipated delays at the customer's premises. We need to make these digital tools generally available to all road users.

Reliability is a short-term concern that is best tackled through investment in cost-effective digital technologies that take advantage of the equipment we have already acquired: satnavs and mobile phones. Investments in civil engineering technologies – shifting earth, pouring concrete, rolling tarmac – are labour-intensive and costly. We need to be critical and realistic in our appraisal of the benefits of such schemes. Realism requires that we base our analysis on what we really expect to happen as the result of an investment, which will include changes in land use and value. We need models to appraise such investments that incorporate changes in land use that contribute to economic growth, as I will discuss further in chapter 7.

Chapter 3

Peak car

The twentieth century was the age of the motor car. As incomes grew, so did car ownership and use. But as we moved into the twenty-first century, this growth ceased and is unlikely to resume. In this chapter I explain why.

We saw in chapter 1 that there has been no growth in average daily travel for the past twenty years. This needs to be explained. Three-quarters of the average distance travelled in Britain is by car (including both drivers and passengers), so it is not unexpected that we find that per capita car use has stabilized (at about 4,000 miles a year). This stability of per capita car use is found in many other developed economies, including the US, where growth ceased well before the financial crisis of 2007–8. This phenomenon is known as 'peak car', although it might better be termed 'plateau car', since the established feature is a cessation of growth. There is a suggestion in some countries of a peak followed by a small decline, but the latter may be a short-term response to the recession.

There are a number of factors that contribute to this cessation of growth, both of per capita car use and of travel by all modes. We discussed one of these in chapter 1: we have run out of technologies that would allow us to go faster.

A second factor is that, with good means of transport available, we have enough daily travel to meet our needs and so do not have to travel further. We can say that our demand for travel has 'saturated'. Demand saturation is a general phenomenon. For instance, ownership of many kinds of home appliance, such as washing machines and fridge-freezers, exceeds 90 per cent, so the markets for such products are largely saturated, with demand arising only from the need for a replacement and from population growth.

In the context of daily travel, 80 per cent of urban households in Britain have three or more large supermarkets within a fifteen-minute drive, and 60 per cent have four or more. So if you have three or four supermarkets within a fifteen-minute drive, would you bother to travel further to have a fourth or fifth choice? If not, then your personal demand for travel to go to supermarkets has saturated – you have enough. Such saturation has come about through the growth of car ownership, on the one hand, and, on the other, through the supermarket chains opening new stores, thus improving accessibility. Both these processes have largely come to an end, however: nearly all households that can drive a car and want one, have one; and the supermarkets have already opened more large stores than are commercially viable.

As well as supermarkets, there is evidence that most people in Britain have a good choice of many regularly used services, provided they have use of a car or good public transport. These include family doctors, hospitals and primary and secondary schools. The implication of good levels of choice is a lack of need to travel further to seek additional choice. To state this in general terms: access and choice increase with the square of the speed of travel (because what you can get to in a given amount of time is defined by the area of a circle whose radius is proportional to the speed of travel, the area being proportional to the square of the radius, as we recall from school mathematics); but choice is subject to diminishing marginal utility (the term used by economists to reflect the successively reducing value of an extra amount of anything you might want). This combination – of choice increasing with the square of the speed but subject to diminishing marginal utility – generates a saturation effect, consistent with the evidence summarized above.

Not all demand for daily travel is subject to saturation, however. An important exception arises from the imbalance in the housing market. If demand and supply were in balance, people could generally find the kind of accommodation they needed within their neighbourhoods – when they wanted to upsize or downsize, for instance. But because demand for housing exceeds supply in many parts of the country, people take advantage of improved transport links to seek homes they can afford further afield, as discussed in the previous chapter.

Both technological constraints that prevent faster travel and demand saturation apply to travel by all modes. Other factors apply specifically to car use, limiting growth and causing a shift to other modes.

Deferred maturity

One general phenomenon found in many developed economies is declining car use by young people, and by young men in their twenties particularly. One way of seeing this is from the decreasing levels of driving licence holding: 83 per cent of English men in their twenties held a licence in the early 1990s; in 2014 the equivalent figure was 63 per cent. A number of factors are at work here. Disposable income is limited as young people defer employment by staying in education longer (with the need to repay student loans); also, rent needs to be paid while saving for the deposit on a home. Car ownership is expensive compared with concessionary travel on buses, advance rail fares, car sharing and car clubs. Those who require their own car to get to work will find the money, but those who can cycle or use public transport tend to put off car ownership or avoid it altogether.

More generally, we are seeing what may be termed 'deferred maturity', a consequence of increasing longevity. Life expectancy – how long on average we may expect to live – is increasing quickly: by two years for every decade that passes. As well as contributing to an ageing population, more years of life ahead allow midlife maturity to be postponed. A key indicator is the average age at which mothers have their children, which has been increasing steadily in Britain for the past forty years to reach thirty years of age. This has allowed more time in education, with 40 per cent of those aged 25–34 having at least a degree-level qualification.

Urban lifestyles for which the car is not a requirement are fostered by higher education on urban university campuses followed by city-based employment where the better jobs (and the cultural and social attractions) are found. Urban living is also facilitated by smartphones – the mobile internet – which provide way-finding and information about bus and rail services and the vast range of leisure and retail opportunities. Dating apps such as Tinder, which allow new friends to be made, offer most choice in high-density urban environments. The prime example of high-density urban living is London, which I will discuss in the next chapter.

An important uncertainty about future demand for travel is the extent to which families with young children will opt to continue urban living or will move to the sub-urbs, where the car becomes more attractive. There is emerging evidence that the attitudes of young people are changing in two significant respects: they have learnt how to use a public transport system that, at least in urban areas and along intercity routes, is improving and resulting in generally positive experiences; and the reallocation of road space away from cars – bus lanes, good walking environments, wide pavements and cycle lanes – makes car journeys longer and makes people more likely to prefer the alternatives.

The shift of the economy from manufacturing to services has led to growth in high-quality jobs in city centres, which offer the attractions of business den-sity: sharing space, facilities, knowledge; matching along supply chains; and learning by seeing what others are doing. Edge-of-town business parks are now less appealing. Accordingly, more business travel is from city centre to city centre, for which rail is convenient, rather than to out-of-town locations, where a car might be necessary. One significant contributor to decreased car travel by men in Britain was a sharp fall in company car use arising from a large increase in tax on fuel pro-vided for private use. On the other hand, women have been driving more in recent years: a reflection of more driving licence holders in successive cohorts of older women.

Forecasts

Taking into account all these factors that contribute to the cessation of growth of per capita car use in Britain and other developed countries, it would be hard to conclude that growth would be likely to resume in the future. So any central case or business-as-usual projection of future car use, and future travel by all surface modes, should hold constant average distance travelled. Alternative cases or scenarios might postulate circumstances that depart from this assumption.

The Department for Transport operates a National Transport Model, which it uses to forecast future travel demand, as part of making the case for new investment in the transport system. However, the department is not yet persuaded by the evidence for cessation of growth of per capita car use. Its model forecasts continued increases, thereby overstating the case for investment in the Strategic Road Network, where expenditure of £15 billion is planned over the next five years. We will return to the matter of transport models and forecasts in subsequent chapters.

If, as I argue, average distance travelled is likely to hold steady, then it follows that total travel demand will in future be driven by population growth, which in Britain is quite rapid. A further 10 million inhabitants are expected by 2040. Their travel needs will have to be met, but the pattern of the growth of demand will depend on where these people live. To the extent that they are housed on greenfield sites, on the edge of existing towns and villages, or in new settlements, they will want cars, and accordingly road construction will be needed. This is illustrated by the example of the garden city planned at Bicester, which I mentioned in chapter 2.

On the other hand, to the extent the additional population is housed within existing urban areas – on brownfield sites, in gaps in streets or at higher density in existing housing – the scope for additional car use is limited, and investment in public transport will be more important than investment in road construction. I will discuss this in the next chapter.

Chapter 4

Green cities

Cities have re-emerged in recent decades as the main locations of economic and population growth. People are attracted to successful cities. But there is little scope to accommodate growth of car use, so investment in urban public transport has become increasingly important. This helps mitigate greenhouse gas emissions from transport, so high-density cities are 'greener' than lower-density suburbs, as I explain in this chapter.

The pattern of human habitation has been shaped by the development of transport systems, which in turn have depended on the evolution of transport technologies. The crucial factor has been the increase in speed made possible by harnessing fossil fuel energy. Two hundred years ago, nearly all travel was on foot, which meant that most people had to live close to where they worked, and so had limited choice of employment, dwellings, markets and other facilities. Rising incomes made possible the widespread adoption of successive technological innovations – bicycles, buses, trams, trains, motorized two-wheelers and cars – that permit faster travel and hence allow access to a wider geographical area than is possible on foot.

For each successive development of transport technology, there was a corresponding kind of city, but the relationship was mutual and path dependent, in that the previous growth of the city shaped and constrained the subsequent transport options. We can distinguish different classes of city according to population density. 'Walking cities' were the major urban form for 8,000 years, and substantial parts of the central areas of many major cities retain this character: dense mixed-use areas no more than 5 kilometres across. 'Transit cities' developed from 1850 to 1950 based on trams, buses and trains, allowing them to spread from dense centres 20–30 kilometres along rail corridors. From the 1950s onwards, 'automobile cities' could spread further, at low density, to 50–80 kilometres.

Investments in a succession of new transport technologies that allow higher speeds of travel have permitted greater access within the time available for travel, and this in turn has offered increased opportunities and choices of employment, residence, shopping, leisure and educational facilities, and so forth, within cities, their suburbs and beyond. But this increased dispersion has come at the cost of increased energy consumption and greenhouse gas emissions.

Transport accounts for over 60 per cent of global oil consumption and about a quarter of energy-related carbon dioxide emissions. Transport has been seen as more problematic than other areas of the economy when it comes to reducing greenhouse gas emissions. Most emphasis has been placed on new technologies, and particularly on electric propulsion, where the present state of battery technology limits widespread adoption.

There is, however, emerging evidence that future growth in car travel may be less than was previously assumed, because of global urbanization at population densities that limit car use. UK travel and transport statistics are exceptionally extensive, permitting us to track developments in London in particular, and we can use these as a case study to exemplify changes in travel patterns as a consequence of population growth at increasing density. As I will explain, a marked shift away from car use is already underway in London – the result of policies that respond to population growth by investing in public transport, especially rail, and by measures to constrain car use. This decrease in car use will significantly help to mitigate transport-related greenhouse gas emissions.

London – a city with a historic centre and mature suburbs – has no greenfield sites for building on, but it does have considerable brownfield land. London has not attempted to increase road capacity in recent years, and has in fact allocated more road space to bus and cycle lanes and to pedestrians, with the result that both car traffic and the number of trips have declined somewhat over the past two decades. Because the population has been growing, the share of all journeys that are taken by car has declined – down from a peak of 50 per cent around 1990 to 36 per cent currently – while public transport use has increased correspondingly, as shown in figure 2. Walking trips have changed little while cycling has grown, but from a low base.

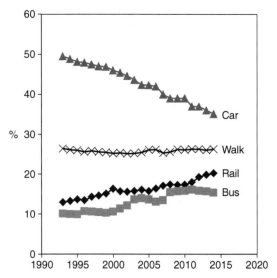

Figure 2. Share of journeys in London by mode of travel.

On the present central-case projection, London's population is expected to grow to 11.3 million by 2050 (from 8.6 million now). To cope with this growth, investments have been made in the public transport system, and further substantial investments are planned in additional rail capacity, but there is no intention to significantly increase road capacity. On this basis, I expect car use in London to decline to about 27 per cent of all trips by the middle of the century, which would be less than half the level of car use in Britain as a whole. Figure 3 shows my estimate of the share of journeys made by car in London over the period 1950–2050. This exemplifies the concept of 'peak car in the big city': a marked peak is seen, in contrast to the concept of peak car at national level, which is more 'plateau car', as discussed in the previous chapter.

There is evidence from two other UK cities, Birmingham and Manchester, that car use in their centres is

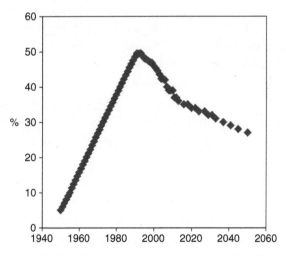

Figure 3. Share of journeys by car in London 1950–2050.

declining. There is also evidence for declining car use per capita, and a rise in public transport use, in the main Australian cities since 2003–4. Comparable, well-documented data is at present limited for large cities in other countries, although anecdotal evidence suggests similar developments are underway.

The global population is expected to increase from 7.0 billion now, half of whom live in urban areas, to 9.3 billion by 2050, according to the UN's 'medium variant' case. Population growth is becoming mainly an urban phenomenon, concentrated in the developing world and resulting in larger cities. At present, some 40 per cent of the world's urban population resides in cities of a million or more people, and this figure is projected to increase to 47 per cent by 2025.

It is generally assumed that car ownership in the developing economies will increase as incomes rise, following a trajectory similar to that in the developed economies. However, population growth and urbanization mean that higher-density cities, where the car is less useful, are likely to become more prevalent. Accordingly, there is the possibility that developing cities with relatively low car ownership at present could avoid the pronounced peak in car use seen in London, moving instead directly to a more sustainable level of car use, avoiding unnecessary investment in vehicles and undesirable emissions of greenhouse gases and pollutants.

Achieving sustainable cities

My proposition is that for a low-to-medium-density city of around 10 million people, limiting the car's share of journeys to less than 30 per cent of journeys will allow the travel needs of the population to be met without excessive traffic congestion and with substantially reduced greenhouse gas emissions. Experience in London suggests that the key policy requirement to achieve such an outcome is investment in rail systems. Also needed are constraints on car use to avoid congestion that detracts from the efficient functioning of essential urban road traffic.

Rail routes – whether underground or overground, classic heavy rail or light rail metros or trams – serve to move commuters to and from work in central business districts as well as provide for journeys while at work, speedily and reliably. A major revival of urban rail is currently underway worldwide for this reason. Because rail is relatively expensive, bus rapid transit (BRT) is a lower-cost alternative: buses operating on dedicated routes that are not impeded by road traffic.

Rail can attract business and professional people out of their cars for work journeys because it is faster and more reliable than the car on congested roads. For example, the new financial centre at Canary Wharf in London's Docklands now accommodates 100,000 well-paid office workers who very largely use new rail routes to get to work, with car trips in the morning peak to the wider Isle of Dogs area accounting for only 10 per cent of the total number of journeys. It is much harder to attract such people onto buses that are no faster than car travel, as well as often being uncomfortably crowded. So cities that rely on buses for public transport tend to suffer from detrimental traffic congestion.

Because roads are open to all vehicles that wish to use them, they tend to be congested at times of peak use in dense urban areas. A successful city needs a street network that gives priority to those functions for which rail is not an alternative: buses, taxis, goods delivery, construction and emergency vehicles. The simplest means of achieving this is to control on-street parking during working hours, whether by prohibition or by charging, since car trips are not made without the assurance of parking at both ends of the journey. Traffic management techniques using coordinated traffic signals are a valuable additional measure for limiting congestion.

Both parking controls and traffic management can be introduced incrementally according to need, with the feasible aim of reducing systemic traffic congestion to an acceptable minimum, so that gridlock is avoided. London also employs congestion charging – a form of road pricing – to manage demand for vehicle use in a central zone. However, introducing such schemes requires political consent, which is often difficult to obtain, and they involve substantial operating and enforcement costs, making it seem unlikely that they will be widely adopted.

Cycling is an important mode in some successful developed cities: it can relieve crowding on public transport and may allow some deferral of investment in expensive new rail routes. Cycling is growing in London, with trips having almost doubled since 2000, albeit from a low base (currently 2 per cent of all trips), and with substantial investment in cycle routes being implemented. Cycling is an important mode in low-income cities, but it then tends to be replaced as incomes rise, first by motorized two-wheelers and then by cars. However, cycling can be revived and can make an important contribution if it is promoted by creating cycle lanes and making low-cost bike hire available. The southern Chinese city of Hangzhou is reported to have the largest public bicycle rental scheme in the world.

Mitigating climate change

Given the expected growth of urban populations, the contribution of urban transport to greenhouse gas emissions is set to increase, and the possibilities for mitigation are consequently being addressed. The main measures comprise improved operational efficiency, promotion of low-carbon technologies, and a drive to improve the attractiveness of walking, cycling and public transport.

While technological and behavioural changes have attracted most attention as ways to mitigate transport greenhouse gas emissions, much depends on how cities respond to growing populations: whether they build upwards at higher densities, as is common in China, or whether they spread out at low densities. In the past, the densities of cities have tended to decline as incomes have risen and people have sought better-quality housing in new suburbs – a seemingly deep-seated counter-urbanization trend that had been the dominant urban force since 1945 in most Western countries.

However, recent experience in Britain suggests that this trend can reverse as people see the attractions of city living. The population of London fell from 8.6 million in 1940 to a minimum of 6.7 million in the late 1980s, as people left an overcrowded and damaged city; but the tide then turned, and London's number of inhabitants recently returned to 8.6 million and is projected, on a central case, to reach 11.3 million by 2050.

More generally, the importance of cities for economic activity is increasingly recognized as a source of 'agglomeration benefits', the term used by economists to describe the benefits obtained by businesses locating near to each other. These comprise 'localization economies', where firms from the same industry benefit through proximity, knowledge spillovers and larger labour pools; and 'urbanization economies', where firms from various industries benefit through concentration of shared resources.

If urban population density increases, catchment areas shrink, whether for schools or supermarkets, which in turn makes the slow modes of cycling and walking potentially more practicable. Walking is facilitated by improvements to the pedestrian environment that enhance the quality of city life. Urban life attracts young people seeking economic, social and cultural opportunities, who see fewer attractions in the car. Creation of car-free public spaces facilitates high-quality urban life. Creativity is fostered through knowledge sharing, whether in formal discussions of professional groups or in the subsequent networking and gossip.

To the extent that growth of urban populations leads to increasing densities, this may be expected to inhibit the increase in car use that would otherwise take place – a possibility that needs to be taken into account in projections of transport sector greenhouse gas emissions. I have estimated the impact both of peak car nationally and of peak car in the big city for UK transport sector carbon emissions using the online '2050 calculator'. (This tool was issued by the Department for Energy and Climate Change to explore possible approaches to meeting the target set in law to reduce UK greenhouse gas emissions by at least 80 per cent by 2050.)

For each sector of the energy economy, the calculator considers four trajectories, reflecting increasing efforts to reduce emissions. For domestic passenger transport, the least ambitious case ('Level 1', consistent with current plans) assumes a 9 per cent increase in average distance travelled by 2050, with little change in mode share. The most ambitious trajectory for travel demand ('Level 4') assumes the same per capita distance travelled in 2050 as today, with a reduction in private vehicle use from 83 per cent of total distance travelled in 2007 to 62 per cent in 2050. However, while Level 4 supposes strong policy interventions (although no details are specified), the outcome is in fact consistent with a continuation of the trends discussed above: a continued absence of growth of per capita travel nationally, with growth of the urban population in London and other large cities resulting in a shift away from car use. Level 4 outcomes may therefore be achievable with no additional policy intervention.

The impact on greenhouse gas emissions also depends on the uptake of zero-emission technologies and improvements to the fuel economy of conventional vehicles. For cautious assumptions in this regard, the reduction in transport energy use by 2050 from Level 4 travel demand behaviour is estimated from the calculator to be 60 per cent, compared with 45 per cent for Level 1 behaviour: a significant additional decrease that would contribute usefully to the overall target of an 80 per cent reduction in greenhouse gas emissions by 2050 against a 1990 baseline. Moreover, adding the strong policy interventions envisaged with Level 4 could achieve an outcome close to this target.

The prospects for population growth in London are prompting investment responses that have the helpful effect of mitigating climate change. Plans for substantial investment in rail transport have as their main aims reducing overcrowding on existing rail routes, accommodating the expected growth of passenger numbers, and making land accessible for residential and commercial property development. Such rail investment will contribute to the shift away from car use and thus to a reduction in transport greenhouse gas emissions, although this is not its main purpose. It may generally be the case that such indirect approaches to greenhouse gas reduction are more cost-effective and publicly acceptable than direct approaches such as subsidizing electric vehicles.

What we are seeing in London has wider relevance. Successful cities are dynamic places, economically, socially and culturally. They attract successful businesses. They lure aspiring people to work, study and live. Population densities increase. Far-sighted city authorities see the need to invest in the transport system to meet the mobility needs of the inhabitants and to prioritize rail over road, for speed and reliability, and to mitigate the impact on global warming. Higher population densities also push up the cost of accommodation so that people tend to occupy less living space and so use less energy for space heating, which further mitigates greenhouse gas emissions while such heating still uses fossil fuels.

The peak in the share of journeys taken by car in London, as seen in figure 3, occurred in 1990. This marks a transition between an era in which increasing prosperity was associated with increasing car ownership and use, to one in which increasing prosperity is associated with *decreasing* car use, at least in successful cities. Beyond the more densely populated areas, where there is road space to allow reasonably free flow and opportunities to park at both ends of the journey, car use will continue to be attractive. But I would not expect average car use to increase by much, if at all, in developed economies.

Beyond the developed economies there is scope for growth in car ownership. It was estimated that more than 1 billion motor vehicles populated the earth in 2010, which could increase to 2 billion by as early as 2020, assuming continued rapid growth in ownership in the developing economies. But such growth may not be inevitable given urbanization of populations, the economic attractions of denser cities, unavoidable constraints on car use in dense urban areas, and the possibilities for alternative modes of travel that allow cities like London to prosper. The level of car use in a large city may be only half that in a country as a whole.

The key policy interventions for ensuring efficient travel for the growing populations of successful cities are a rail and/or BRT network to get office workers in city centres out of their cars for work journeys, and constraints on car use to avoid congestion that impedes essential urban road traffic. For cities in developing countries with low current car use, the peak car experience may be avoided and a more sustainable outcome achieved. The future growth of transport sector greenhouse gas emissions could therefore be significantly lower than is generally projected.

Chapter 5

Up in the air

So far we have considered only surface travel by road and rail, the means by which we carry out our daily journeys outside the home, as well as making more occasional longer trips. Let us now turn to air travel. As I will explain, there are some significant parallels between surface and air travel.

The number of passengers travelling through Britain's airports has grown rapidly in recent decades, increasing fivefold between the mid 1970s and 2007, when it reached a peak of 240 million. Numbers then dropped back due to the recession but growth resumed and is projected to continue. The British government set up the Airports Commission to address the need for additional runway capacity. The Commission forecast a doubling of passenger numbers by 2050 as a central estimate, and accordingly proposed a new runway at Heathrow. This growth forecast was based on an econometric model of air travel, developed by the Department for Transport and refined by the Commission. It projects future demand assuming that past statistical relationships continue to apply: relationships between passenger numbers and factors such as personal income, GDP and oil prices, for instance. The conventional wisdom is that there will be substantial future growth in demand for air travel, and there is a presumption that we must invest in additional airport capacity to provide for that demand. However, both the expected growth and the presumption are questionable.

It is illuminating to break down the historic pattern of growth in passenger numbers by market segment. Figure 4 shows passenger numbers between the UK and the US and between the UK and Japan, and it is clearly

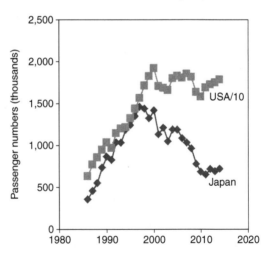

Figure 4. Annual air travel passenger numbers between the UK and Japan and between the UK and the US.

seen that there was strong growth in both cases through to the late 1990s. During that period, it would have been natural to project continued growth into the twenty-first century, whether by visual extrapolation of the trend or by building a formal model. However, growth stopped abruptly, in both markets.

In the case of the US, there has been no growth for fifteen years. The timing of the transition coincided with the 9/11 terrorist attacks, which would naturally deter non-essential air travel. But it is unexpected that growth did not resume after a break. In the case of Japan, passenger numbers halved before bottoming out.

Are these remarkable statistics real, or could this be a statistical artefact? One important development in recent years has been the growth of the airlines based at hub airports in the Middle East. When we fly to Japan, we can go direct from Heathrow to Tokyo or we can travel via Dubai, for instance, which would take longer, because of the need to change planes, but could be cheaper. Might the apparent decline in passenger numbers be the result of the airlines reporting numbers to the intermediate destination rather than the final one? The answer comes from the International Passenger Survey administered by the Office for National Statistics at ports and airports, which asks returning UK residents where they have been, how long they stayed there, and how much they spent. Similar questions are asked of people from other countries returning from a trip to

Britain. From these sources we can track visitor numbers between the UK and Japan, which halved over the same timescale over which airline passenger numbers halved. So this halving of both visitor and passenger numbers is real, not an artefact.

For travel between the UK and US we have 'plateau air travel', and for Japan we have 'peak air travel'. But the US and Japan are not typical market segments. Most segments show continuing growth, which is why the Airports Commission projected a doubling of passenger numbers by the middle of the century. The US and Japan are important and well-established markets, though, and the US in particular is a very large market. It is possible that what we are seeing is evidence of 'market maturity': a general phenomenon that is found with any new product or service that becomes popular, for which demand grows faster than the rate of growth of the economy as a whole, so that growth must eventually slow and stop. At this point we have demand saturation, as discussed in chapter 3.

If the cessation of growth in air travel between the UK and the US and Japan is due to market maturity, it is to be expected that this will also be seen in other market segments in time. It is unlikely that the standard econometric models adequately include the factors contributing to maturity – such models never project the kind of trend shown in figure 4 – so it is important to understand these factors and build them into better models.

Time is one possible constraint on the growth of air travel. We have already discussed the fact that there are many activities that have to be fitted into a day's twenty-four hours, and that this means that the time we can allow ourselves for daily travel is an hour a day on average. For international travel by air, it is not the hours in the day that matter, but the days in the year. Not days of flying time, but days away from responsibilities at home or work. For retired people with empty nests, there may be no such time constraints, but this is not how it is for most of us, although we have little relevant data for this neglected aspect of air travel.

We can see in general terms how time constraints might operate. A British firm might have developed export outlets in the US, perhaps visiting clients quarterly. Then the firm explores opportunities in new markets, leaving less time for visits to the US, where modern telecommunications can substitute to some extent for face-to-face contact with well-established customers. In the case of leisure travel, the time allowed for holidays from work constrains tourism, and the availability of new destinations can take visitors away from old established ones. Once-popular English seaside resorts such as Blackpool saw growth in visitor numbers from the nineteenth century, with the coming of the railways and paid annual holidays, to a peak around 1960, followed by a decline as cheap air travel to more reliably sunny destinations attracted people away. The big drop in passenger numbers between the UK and Japan is due mainly to a fall in inbound leisure visitors from Japan, possibly on account of the attractions of alternative destinations.

Time away from home does not relate straightforwardly to number of flights made. A two-week holiday abroad in one location involves one return flight, whereas two separate weeks away involves two return flights. We have information on the frequency of air travel from the National Travel Survey: not from the seven-day travel diaries described in chapter 1, since these would not capture the relatively rare trips abroad; but from a separate question that has been asked in recent years about the number of times respondents travelled abroad by air in the previous twelve months.

A striking finding is that just over half of those responding did not fly even once in the previous year. I designate these the 'infrequent flyers'. They are a mixed bunch: some fly rarely, some have never flown and some flew frequently in the past but have changed their habits. They are interesting because they could be a reservoir of potential demand for air travel in the future, if their needs could be better met.

We have some knowledge of the characteristics of the infrequent flyers since the National Travel Survey collects personal information about respondents. We find that as incomes rise, the proportion of infrequent flyers falls – consistent with the expectation that budgetary constraints limit air travel. However, 30 per cent of those in the top fifth in terms of income did not fly in the previous year, although presumably they could have afforded at least one trip.

Most of what we know about people who fly comes from passenger surveys at airports, which in Britain are carried out by the Civil Aviation Authority, the airports regulator. But passenger surveys do not pick up many of the infrequent flyers, who by definition are rarely to be found at airports. However, the Civil Aviation Authority has carried out a household survey of attitudes to air travel, which, like the National Travel Survey, includes infrequent flyers. From this we find that the main reason given by this group for not flying is budgetary constraint – cited by almost half.

If budgetary constraint is the main reason for infrequent flyers not travelling abroad, we might expect that more would do so if incomes grow in the future. But incomes would need to grow faster than the costs of travel, which comprise both the cost of flying and the cost of accommodation when abroad. The biggest reason for the rapid growth in air travel over the past twenty years has been the entry of the budget airlines, the low-cost carriers, whose operating efficiency has driven down the price of tickets. For short-haul leisure travel, this price reduction has probably gone as far as it can go: we fly either on the budget airlines or on legacy airlines at similar prices, since this market is highly competitive. There is an open question about the prospects for cheaper long-haul flights. It seems most likely that the economics of long-haul would allow significant price reduction only on the most popular routes. If so, the boost to flying from increased affordability is largely behind us. And in any event, those subject to budgetary constraint would not be likely to undertake the more expensive long-haul trips.

To summarize the prospects for the growth of air travel to and from the UK: on the one hand, we have the possible emergence of market maturity, which would exert a downward influence; and on the other, the possibility that rising incomes may allow more of the infrequent flyers to travel. My judgment is that the former is likely to be the more important factor. If so, the requirement for additional runway capacity may be later than the Airports Commission predicts. But in any event, the uncertainty over future demand is arguably a good deal greater than the Commission believes. This uncertainty feeds through into the economic benefits expected.

Economic benefits

The Commission estimated the economic benefit to Britain of an additional runway at Heathrow to be some £69 billion (net present value), offset by disbenefits and costs that reduce the net benefit to £12 billion. This economic benefit is what the investment would generate, over and above the outcome of what is known as the 'do-minimum' case – the scale and pattern of air travel without an additional runway.

The standard approach of transport economists, outlined in chapter 2, assumes that the main economic benefit of an improvement in the transport system is the saving of travel time. However, this is of limited relevance for air travel since the speed of aircraft has not increased over the past fifty years. Additional runway capacity gives only limited benefits in respect of travel time – reduced delays if an airport is able to operate at less than full capacity, for example – but it does allow an increase in the numbers travelling, with the possibility of more airlines competing for their business and so lower fares. On the other hand, the construction of a new runway has to be paid for by users, which would increase fares. In short, the standard approach is based on notional benefits to users that have a tenuous relationship to the wider economic benefits cited by those who favour new capacity.

The Airports Commission therefore commissioned from consultants a model (known as a spatial computable generalized equilibrium model) to estimate how the benefits of investment would feed through into prices, wages, productivity, business location and the like in the wider economy. The model was used to compare the outcome for the economy if it had the new runway capacity (the 'do-something' case) with the outcome absent that capacity ('do-minimum'). This model is exceptionally complex and the outputs have to be taken on trust since the detailed structure is not publicly available.

While a 250-page description of the modelling exercise has been published, what is not made clear is the basis for the 'do-minimum' case. I infer that a fairly static scenario is assumed, air travel from south-east England being limited by runway capacity constraints but maintaining broadly the existing pattern of use. What has been missed, however, is the likelihood of the market for air travel changing markedly in these circumstances, meaning that we need to consider a dynamic 'do-minimum' scenario.

Most air travel is for leisure: tourism, visiting family and friends. For the UK as a whole, three-quarters of air travel is for leisure purposes. Even at Heathrow, business passengers are a minority: 30 per cent of the total. However, the arguments for additional runway capacity are mainly about the need for more business travel: for UK firms to access new export markets, to encourage inward investment to Britain, and to foster the continued growth of London as a world city for doing business.

The case for additional runway capacity to expand leisure travel is far less evident. Certainly, the retail, hospitality and entertainment sectors would welcome more inbound tourists. But Britain has a substantial negative balance of trade in tourism. The British travelling abroad spend about £30 billion a year, whereas inbound tourists spend about £20 billion. More air travel could worsen this imbalance. Moreover, there is an emerging problem in London, whose performance as a working city is arguably beginning to be adversely affected by the growing scale of tourism, as evidenced by the steady increase in visitor numbers and crowding in the main museums, galleries and other public buildings.

There is ample capacity at Heathrow for the growth of business travel if it displaces leisure travellers. This would happen through normal market forces since business travellers would be willing to pay a premium price for the convenience of using this hub airport. Growing demand from business travellers would be accommodated in part by larger aircraft, such as the Airbus 380, which can carry as many as 600 passengers, and by relocating some short-haul routes used mainly by leisure travellers to other airports. More generally, leisure travellers would consider the wide range of options on offer, as happens already.

If I travel to India on a short business trip for which someone else is paying, I'll fly direct. But if I'm on a longer holiday visit, paying out of my own pocket, I'll consider travelling with one of the airlines based at hubs in the Middle East, which will offer lower prices in exchange for the inconvenience of changing flights en route. At present, I'd leave from Heathrow in both cases, but if growth of business travellers at that airport meant that I'd have to depart from another airport to secure an attractive price, I'd certainly be willing to consider that option. Apart from Heathrow, there are flights at least daily via Middle East hubs from Gatwick and five regional airports, but not yet from Stansted, to the north of London, which has plenty of spare capacity.

If it were easy to decide where to locate a further runway in south-east England, if it were easy to mitigate the noise, air pollution and climate change impacts that would arise, and if it were easy to finance the capital cost from within the private sector (since UK airports are privately, not publicly, owned), then it would be sensible to proceed. But none of these desiderata are easy to fulfil. Moreover, demand for air travel by UK residents may be nearer to maturity than is generally supposed, as I argued earlier. Accordingly, it would be reasonable to defer a decision on a new runway, allowing the market to respond to a capacity constraint.

The Airports Commission's estimate of the economic benefit of a new runway at Heathrow is both notional in its computation and much too large, in my judgment, being based on a 'do-minimum' comparator that fails to recognize the likely market response to a capacity constraint. Britain has an exceptionally competitive market in air travel, including five airports in the London area all under different ownership, plus a multiplicity of vigorously competing airlines. I am not an economist with a strong belief in the efficiency of markets – I'm neither an economist by profession nor a principled believer in markets as the best means of allocating scarce resources – but I do think that we have underestimated the scope for the aviation market to deliver acceptable outcomes if it proves too difficult to gain political and public agreement over the proposed new Heathrow runway.

Chapter 6

Technologies – slow and fast

Technology has always been at the heart of the transport system. New technologies permit faster travel by more people. There is a lot of current excitement about innovations such as driverless cars. In this chapter, I address the fundamental features of transport technologies as these have developed over the past two centuries, the likely impact of the new digital technologies, and what is implied for how we might travel in the future.

Transport technologies are slow to change. After the initial breakthrough of the first vehicle – train, car or plane – development is incremental. However, cumulative incremental development of mechanical and civil engineering technologies can result in huge improvements in performance, reliability and comfort over time. Witness the enormous advance between the Model T Ford – the first mass-produced automobile, which hit the road a century ago – and the modern car. We have seen similar advances on the railways and in the air.

These developments are 'path dependent', in that once we have set out it is hard to switch to what could be a better approach, given the investments already made. So our railways use the same track gauge – the distance between the rails – that was established by the very first commercial railway. On the roads, the investments made in the fuel supply system inhibit a switch to alternative sources such as hydrogen or electric power. There remains, nevertheless, considerable scope for incremental improvement of existing transport technologies. Better internal combustion engine technology will reduce emissions of both carbon dioxide and noxious pollutants; this will be driven by public concern about urban air pollution and by regulation. More efficient aircraft engines will both reduce emissions and lessen the cost of air travel.

One emerging step change away from the traditional road vehicle is the electrification of transport by means of the electric car, which is attractive because it has zero emissions – from the vehicle itself at least. The source of electricity supply would need to be decarbonized if true zero emissions from road transport are to be obtained, which is what would be needed to meet the UK's national target of an 80 per cent reduction in greenhouse gas emissions by 2050. There would also need to be substantial investment in the electricity supply system to make charging points of sufficient capacity widely available.

The main constraint on the rapid deployment of electric cars is the current performance of batteries, which at present are heavy, slow to recharge and have limited energy storage capacity. They are also expensive, currently accounting for around a third of the cost of an electric vehicle. However, the prize for useful innovation is very large, and extensive research and development is underway by specialist battery manufacturers. Incremental improvement, possibly quite rapid, is to be expected, and a technological breakthrough is not out of the question.

Tesla, the US specialist developer of pure electric cars, advertises its Model S as being capable of a range of over 330 miles on one charge. Such a range depends on how the car is driven and it may be significantly less in practice. For the routine short commute to work and back, home charging suffices. But for a longer trip there is the question of where to recharge. While the availability of public recharging points is growing in many cities, concerns about where to recharge tend to limit purchases of electric cars.

One answer to such 'range anxiety' is the hybrid vehicle, whose popularity has been growing rapidly. Hybrids have both an internal combustion engine and an electric motor, the former being used both to charge the battery and to drive the road wheels when battery charge is low. A more recent innovation is the plug-in hybrid, which can be charged at home overnight, to take advantage of low-taxed electricity.

Electric and hybrid cars – 'ultra-low emission vehicles' – are more expensive to buy than their conventional counterparts but tend to be taxed less and have lower fuel costs, so they are greener and cheaper to run. The government claims that the UK already has the largest market for ultra-low emission vehicles in the European Union, and the fourth largest in the world, and is committed to ensuring almost every car and van is a zero emission vehicle by 2050.

However, these new road vehicle technologies will not allow us to travel faster, nor do they affect congestion. So electric and hybrid cars will not change the fundamentals of how we travel. Similarly, in the air the speed of aircraft will not increase, being limited by considerations of fuel economy, noise and emissions, and by the sound barrier. Concorde, the elegant supersonic airliner, proved to be a technological and commercial dead end.

On the railways, there is some scope for faster travel at higher speeds. HS2 – the planned new rail route north out of London to connect to the cities of the Midlands and the North – will run at up to 250 miles per hour, resulting in a useful reduction in journey times, which, it is hoped, will translate into economic benefits for these cities. Faster than high-speed rail running on conventional tracks is Maglev, a technology that uses magnetic levitation to move vehicles along a guideway without touching the ground. The reduced friction potentially allows very high speeds. One Maglev system operates in Shanghai, between the airport and city centre, covering nineteen miles in eight minutes, a faster, albeit more expensive, alternative to the metro. While trains using high-speed routes can continue on conventional tracks where investment to upgrade is not justified, Maglev vehicles are limited to purpose-built guideways. Inflexibility and high construction costs are likely to limit deployment.

Generally, vehicle and infrastructure technologies are developing incrementally, spurred by competitive manufacturers that operate globally and by construction companies operating mainly nationally. Mechanical and civil engineering technologies are inherently slow to evolve. Legislation and regulation governing safety and environment both spur and constrain innovation, so that change is measured rather than disruptive.

Digital technologies

What a contrast to the digital technologies, where development is typically fast and often disruptive. So what happens when the digital meets transport? The beginnings were a couple of decades ago when the term 'telematics' was coined to designate the application of information and telecommunication technologies to road transport. The current term is 'intelligent transport systems', which covers rail applications as well (aviation has long utilized these technologies).

Initial developments were fairly cautious, but the pace is accelerating. The most straightforward are bolt-on devices, satnav in particular, which is now pretty ubiquitous, whether integrated into the vehicle by the manufacturer, as a free-standing device, or as included in a mobile phone. Satnav provides optimal routes plus alternative options to deal with delays.

Digital devices that govern vehicle behaviour require careful design and are now appearing in top-of-the-range models. Adaptive cruise control, employing laser or radar sensors, automatically adjusts the vehicle speed to keep a safe distance from the vehicle ahead. Lane-keeping systems use a forward-facing camera to view lane markings, to alert the driver if the car is drifting out of its lane and assist in steering back. Self-parking systems allow a vehicle to park hands-free. Such devices are contributing to a reduced role for the driver, which ultimately could lead to driverless vehicles (also known as autonomous or self-driving vehicles). The crucial transition is from high automation to full automation.

The other – direct – route to full automation is being pioneered by Google, which is building and testing on the streets prototype vehicles that make no provision for a driver: no steering wheel or brakes. This approach uses map and sensor information, together with soft-ware that predicts what nearby objects, such as cyclists, might do next, to set the speed and course of the car. The reliability of such predictions is clearly crucial, including when it comes to predicting unusual events.

Whichever route to autonomous vehicles is taken, stringent requirements will need to be met, involving extensive on-road testing, before drivers are allowed to take their hands off the wheel. Driverless vehicles will need to be demonstrably safer than conventional vehicles. In principle, this should be achievable given that road traffic accidents in Britain were responsible for 1,775 deaths and 193,000 injuries in 2014. The pre-dominant contributory factor is human error, respon-sible for 94 per cent of all such collisions, in particular failure to look properly and to judge another person's path or speed. Technology should be capable of doing better than humans, although there will be tricky judgements for the driverless vehicles to make: a paper bag blowing across the road or something more substantial, a child's ball or the child itself. Accidents would still happen and there will need to be clarifica-tion of civil and criminal liabilities should an autono-mous vehicle be in a collision. The responsibilities of vehicle manufacturers and insurers will need to be addressed, and also of drivers where they might take control, but provided a sufficiently low accident rate can be achieved, an acceptable outcome should be possible, not least on account of a reduction in insurance claims.

One other important concern is cybersecurity, particularly where a vehicle acquires digital data from its environment. There is scope for both vehicle-to-vehicle and roadside-to-vehicle communications, to improve safety and efficiency of using the road network. Functions of the vehicle that are critical to safety – such as steering and braking – would need to be 'fail safe' in case of interference with such communications. More generally, the software used in driverless vehicles would need to achieve levels of error well below current standards, and software suppliers would need to accept liability for the consequences of their errors, which at present they do not do.

Beyond such dedicated forms of communication, the use of the internet to schedule vehicles and their users has led to striking developments recently. Most notable are on-demand ride services, such as that offered by Uber, whose apps both allow users to summon and pay for a vehicle and allow drivers to find the best route. Other uses of the internet include enabling ride-sharing on intercity trips, such as offered by Liftshare and BlaBlaCar, and the hiring of private parking spaces to others. The bike-hire schemes available in big cities depend on digital communications to effect payment and return arrangements for what is a decidedly mechanical technology.

An emerging concept is 'mobility-as-a-service', in which travellers use services, rather than personal vehicles, for transportation. This is made possible by internet-based services and by the opportunities to link different modes of transport into seamless trip chains, with bookings and payments managed by a single service provider. With this approach, personal car ownership would take on far less importance than it currently does, since vehicles would be shared.

Sharing

There is growing interest generally in the idea of sharing. The 'sharing economy' takes advantage of the internet to bring excess capacity into use, whether underused assets (private cars, spare bedrooms) or labour (people willing to put in a few hours of effort). This is a disruptive economic force that unlocks new sources of supply at lower cost, which benefits consumers but could be detrimental to traditional suppliers.

For transport, the sharing economy can offer efficiency improvements. Ride sharing involves people sharing the car and the cost, whether colleagues on regular journeys to work or new friends on one-off longer trips. Ride sharing improves the occupancy of cars – a real efficiency gain for the road network – and reduces carbon and other emissions per capita.

However, the main transport opportunities seem to be in shared ownership, taking advantage of the fact that most private cars are parked for more than 95 per cent of the time. Car rental by the day is familiar. Car clubs allow people to avoid owning their own car when their needs are limited. One model requires vehicles to be returned to the point of origin, normally close to where you live. Another approach allows return anywhere within a defined area. This kind of short-term car sharing is in competition with taxis, where costs have been reducing under the influence of Uber. Driverless cars – essentially taxis with robot drivers – may be particularly suited to ownership models other than the standard private car, since such autonomous vehicles could travel when empty to where needed by the next user.

A number of major car manufacturers have announced Airbnb-style schemes that allow car owners to earn money by renting out their new vehicles to others. This is a response to the disruption of traditional consumer sectors by the concept of sharing and by the declining use of cars on the part of the urban young – because of both the costs of ownership and the alternative modes of transport that are increasingly available in successful cities.

It makes sense to share underused assets where that is convenient for those concerned. But how much difference would car sharing in all its forms make to road use, if its growth continues? The prospects seem varied.

Car sharing would reduce personal ownership but car use would be more intensive, which might make little difference to overall traffic. Roadside parking would be reduced if personal ownership declines, but this would be largely in residential neighbourhoods where on-street parking is permitted, so the impact on urban traffic congestion in city centres would not be great. However, driverless cars owned by individuals could be programmed to cruise round the block while waiting for the owner to finish their business – in effect 'parking' while on the move, which would contribute to congestion and accordingly would need to be regulated. Perhaps driverless vehicles without an occupant, other than taxis, would need to be banned in city centres.

Car sharing could reduce car use since those who do not own their own personal vehicles tend to make less use of cars. Ride sharing could reduce car use, or it might take people away from public transport, particularly rail on intercity trips. Driverless taxis might allow cheaper fares, robot drivers being lower cost than humans, which would increase demand, but the impact on congestion would depend on how much reduction in private ownership took place, and also on whether the distance between vehicles could safely be reduced. Altogether, the impact of car sharing on road use seems unlikely to be substantial. In the medium term, it could go either way, depending on whether or not increased demand outweighs increased efficiency.

As well as facilitating these various forms of car sharing, digital technologies are of increasing importance in public transport. Real-time information at bus stops and railway stations reduces uncertainty and anxiety. Websites and apps on smartphones allow trip planning and ticket booking. Payment for tickets using contactless cards is fast and convenient, as with Oyster cards and standard bank or credit cards in London. The doubling of national rail passenger numbers over the past twenty years, and the growth of public transport use in London in particular, have undoubtedly been aided by these digital innovations.

Digital technologies are central to the Urban Traffic Management systems that function in our cities, out of sight and generally out of mind, sensing the build-up of traffic and tweaking the timings of the traffic signals to optimize flow. The potential of London's well-developed system was seen during the 2012 Olympic Games, when there were major traffic flow redirections and yet gridlock was avoided.

Beyond boosting use of public transport, there has been a long-running but inconclusive debate about how the increasing market penetration of digital technologies affects travel behaviour. On the one hand, telecommunications could substitute for travel, as when online shopping replaces the personal visit – although a van still has to deliver the goods, and the time saved on the shopping trip might be used for a journey of a different kind, consistent with the fixed average travel time discussed in chapter 1. On the other hand, the larger networks of friends and colleagues made possible by email and social media generate more opportunities to travel for face-to-face contact, important for establishing trust and reaffirming friendship – trips that are made easier by the ability to keep in touch with home and work while away.

Apart from such direct impacts of digital technologies on travel, there are indirect effects, one of which is the way the mobile internet facilitates high-density urban living where the car is not part of the lifestyle, as discussed in chapter 4.

Tortoise and hare

An often helpful way of thinking about new innovations is known as the 'hype cycle', devised by the consultants Gartner. What is seen over time is a 'technology trigger', leading to a 'peak of inflated expectations', followed by a 'trough of disillusionment', then an upward 'slope of enlightenment', reaching a 'plateau of productivity'. With driverless vehicles we are arguably at the inflated peak of expectations currently, but that does not preclude benefits in the long run.

So far, the thrust of my argument is that although businesses based on free-standing digital technologies can grow quickly and be disruptive, when applied to the slow-to-evolve transport technologies, it is the tortoise that holds back the hare. The one somewhat potentially disruptive innovation that may already be underway is on-demand ride services such as Uber displacing traditional taxis – but this is disruptive only for the black cab drivers, not for passengers or for road users generally. On-demand ride services might replace buses on routes with low occupancy – disruptive for incumbent operators but possibly beneficial for users.

However, looking further ahead it is possible to envisage a more substantial change, what might be termed a 'shared–squared–driverless' scenario: shared ownership of driverless vehicles with shared use. So rather than one or two occupants, the aim would be to fill the vehicle at peak times with passengers travelling in the same direction. This would reduce urban traffic congestion through high occupancy requiring fewer vehicles, with one study suggesting that a single such vehicle could replace nine conventional cars in a US city. Uber has introduced uberPOOL, a shared taxi service with lower fares, and uberHOP, which facilitates sharing along commuter routes at peak times. Their success will depend on the ability to match enough passengers going in the same direction, and also on the willingness of people to share.

If priority were given to shared–squared–driverless vehicles through road pricing or similar demand-control measures, it might be possible to avoid urban traffic congestion while offering speedy and reliable door-to-door travel. This would be facilitated by some central oversight of such vehicles to minimize conflicts and maximize efficient use of the road network (analogous to air traffic control). The outcome would allow the car to compete with rail in urban areas, in terms of speed and reliability, and could help cities without rail infrastructure better meet the mobility needs of their citizens.

Such a shared–squared–driverless vehicle scenario, if feasible in practice, would take quite some time to be implemented, in terms of both the technology and a business model to make the transition. For the time being, we have two modes of transport in competition. Roads allow door-to-door travel at a time of your choosing and are open to all (provided you have a driving licence, a vehicle and pay requisite charges) and are therefore prone to congestion at times of peak demand. Rail offers station-to-station journeys according to a timetable, avoiding congestion delays under normal operations but prone to crowding at peak times.

We have seen a resurgence of rail travel, both urban and inter-urban, in recent years as roads have become more congested and as city centre activity has grown. The immediate challenge is to increase the capacity of the existing rail network to meet growing demand and, at the same time, to improve the quality of the journey through seamless planning and ticketing. Transport for London, a world-leading operator, has ambitious plans to meet these objectives, and other city regions in Britain are beginning to follow suit.

Chapter 7

The future of travel

In this chapter I draw together findings and concepts from previous chapters to suggest how our travel needs are likely to be met in the future. Economic and population growth will require continued transport investment. The challenge is to understand the consequences of the different kinds of investment so that the outcomes meet society's needs.

Future trends in travel patterns will depend both on changes in individual behaviour and on wider demographic and technological developments. A key change in behaviour in the developed economies has been the end of the historic relationship whereby growing incomes led to increasing distance travelled, mainly through more widespread car ownership. Vehicle ownership in Britain is still growing, partly on account of population growth and partly because of additional cars per household, but the latter are probably responsible for only a relatively small increase in total mileage.

As we saw in chapter 1, the pattern of daily travel in Britain has been broadly stable over the past twenty years. On average we make about a thousand journeys a year, travelling for about an hour a day and covering about 7,000 miles a year, mostly to meet everyday needs (this excludes air travel). Although the future is uncertain, a reasonable central assumption is that this stable pattern will remain. (Alternative assumptions would generate other scenarios worth considering.) This means that future total demand for travel will be driven by population growth, and that the future pattern of demand growth will depend on whether the additional inhabitants are housed on greenfield sites or within existing urban areas. The revival of cities as sources of economic dynamism, as well as places of cultural and social vibrancy, serves to constrain car use and enhance sustainability.

Transport technologies generally change slowly and incrementally, as discussed in the previous chapter. But even significant changes in vehicle technology, such as electric propulsion or driverless cars, will not change the fundamental feature of the road system: that it is open to all and so tends to be congested in and near urban areas at times of peak demand. The crucial technological distinction for surface transport has always been between the open road and the closed railway. In densely populated cities, rail in all its forms competes effectively with the car on congested roads, particularly for work-related journeys.

Future changes in transport technologies will increasingly be brought about by developments in the digital sphere – apps that facilitate easier use of public transport, for example. More generally, mobile internet facilitates city living by the urban young, for whom the car is not central to the lifestyle. Having fewer cars in the centres of cities and towns allows more interactions between people, with benefits that are economic, social and cultural.

A combination of behavioural, demographic and technological changes is contributing to a marked shift away from the car in London, an example of a successful big city with a growing population. As we saw in chapter 4, the peak of car use is well behind us, with a marked fall from 50 per cent of all trips in around 1990, when the population was at a minimum following half a century of decline, to 36 per cent currently, and that share is projected to fall further: to 27 per cent by the middle of the century with current policies and population projections.

The peak of car use in London, as shown in figure 3, reflects a transition that can be ascribed to a number of changed behaviours: from travel demand driven by rising incomes to population growth being the main determinant; from an association between growing prosperity and growing car ownership in the twentieth century to the twenty-first-century association between growing prosperity and decreasing car use in successful cities; and from an era of steadily increasing travel, which started with the coming of the railways that harnessed the energy of fossil fuels to allow faster movement than walking pace, to the current era in which this growth in distance travelled has now ended, since there is little prospect of technologies that will allow safe and sustainable travel at yet higher speeds.

The peak shown in figure 3 would not have been forecast in advance. A transport planner in the 1980s, thinking about future travel patterns in London, would have predicted continued population decline and continued growth of car use, albeit saturating at some point in the future. An econometric model based on past trends would generate the same kind of projection. However, such models cannot take account of the kinds of behavioural change that underlie the peak car phenomenon, at least until well after those changes have occurred. Reliance on such models for planning is therefore problematic.

Forecasting the future

The Department for Transport has built a National Transport Model that it uses to inform national investment and policy decisions. Forecasts of road traffic are regularly published, and these are then used to support local transport investment proposals. However, those responsible for the model have not yet recognized that car use in London peaked twenty-five years ago. Their forecasts for car traffic in London project growth of as much as 37 per cent by 2040 (depending on the scenario), which is very hard to reconcile both with the downward trend in London's car traffic seen over the past twenty years and with the policy intentions of both London's mayor and Transport for London: to improve but not enlarge the road network, and to invest substantially in the rail system.

The National Transport Model also failed to predict the growth in demand for rail travel: the doubling of passenger numbers over the past twenty years, after a long period of gentle decline. And I mentioned in chapter 5 how the Department for Transport's model of demand for air travel would not have predicted the cessation of growth observed in travel between the UK and the US and Japan.

The general problem with all such models is that their construction incorporates *past* relationships between travel parameters and factors that are believed to influence travel behaviour, such as income, GDP, oil prices, taxes and technological advances. The implicit assumption is that the future will be similar to the past, change being incremental and continuous. However, the shifts in behaviour we have observed in recent years show that trends can change direction quite markedly. This suggests that how we choose to travel may be more open to influence than is usually supposed.

Modellers rely on established relationships between key parameters: relationships based on historical data. When such relationships are changing, the emerging evidence is generally quite limited. So if the modellers simply weigh the available evidence by numbers of relevant published reports, there is an inevitable 'bias against the future', which is undesirable when we use models to make investment decisions whose benefits will be well into the future. One approach is to develop scenarios that explore a wider range of possible futures, which the modellers responsible for the National Transport Model have begun to do. But this complicates the task of the decision makers.

A traditional approach to decision-making has been to 'predict and provide': predict demand and make provision for the expected growth by investing. Over-prediction of demand results in over-investment, which as well as being costly in economic terms can be costly environmentally: concreting over the countryside, polluting the air and generating noise. We therefore need models that recognize evidence of changing trends in behaviour if we are to make realistic forecasts of future travel demand. We also need to estimate the benefits of investment in new infrastructure to meet growing demand based on evidence of how travel behaviour changes in response to such investment.

The main benefit from transport investments, in the view of transport economists, is the saving of travel time, as I discussed in chapter 2. But average travel time doesn't change: it has remained at around an hour a day since humans settled in farming communities. Evidently, in the long run there are no time savings that would allow more productive work or valued leisure, despite transport investments costing many billions of pounds of public money, all justified by calculation of notional time savings.

What we get for such investment is faster travel that allows more access to land that can be developed economically. The regeneration of London's Docklands is a clear example, where we see (literally, from the elevated tracks of the Docklands Light Railway) commercial and residential properties constructed by private sector developers to accommodate a growing economy and a growing population. However, the value of this development, as reflected in enhanced land and property prices, is not included in the standard approach to investment appraisal employed by economists, since this would double-count benefits already presumed to be included as time savings.

So transport economists prefer to measure the value of a proposed long-lived transport investment in terms of notional short-run time savings rather than expected increases in the long-run market value of real estate. This is not sensible in principle and is misleading for decision makers. Let us consider some examples of problematic investment decisions.

Rail investments

HS2, the planned new rail route from London to the cities of the Midlands and the North, is a controversial project that has generated both strong support and strong opposition, particularly from those who expect to be adversely affected by the environmental impact. The cost of construction is very substantial: of the order of £50 billion. What is the economic case?

Demand for rail travel has been growing rapidly, with passenger numbers doubling over the twenty years since the industry was privatized. Has this growth arisen because of or despite privatization? Probably both: the train operating companies have invested in new rolling stock, which attracts customers; but growth has also been the result of road congestion, digital technologies that allow productive work on rail journeys, the shift of the economy from manufacturing to business services located in city centres, and more people living in cities without a car.

We can expect demand for rail travel to continue to grow, driven both by population increase and by the attractions of an improving network that offers fast and reliable travel. There is therefore a good case for investing in track, stations, signalling and rolling stock. Additional capacity on existing routes is not controversial, despite weekend interruptions to services, and can be cost-effective if space for enlargement exists. Longer trains and longer platforms, with a smaller proportion of first class seats, is one such approach, although the decade-long modernization of the West Coast Main Line, completed in 2008, was problematic, involving delays and cost overruns. Most rail investment involves improving existing routes, or occasionally reviving dis-used track, for mixed passenger and freight use. The main exception is HS2: a new-build high-speed route for fast passenger trains only.

The development of HS2 is being carried forward by a government-owned company. Legislation agreed by parliament is necessary to secure powers to con-struct the new route. The strategic case for HS2, pub-lished in 2013, argues that this offers a step change in north–south connectivity, at a cost for a high-speed line of 9 per cent more than a conventional railway. Travel time from London to Birmingham, for example, would be reduced from 81 minutes to 49 minutes. Long-distance trips transferred to the new line would free up capacity on existing routes for additional com-muter services.

An important part of the strategic case for HS2 is the economic case. On the standard approach to transport cost–benefit analysis, where the main eco-nomic benefit is time saving through faster travel, the benefit-to-cost ratio is estimated to be 1.7 for the first phase (London to Birmingham) and 2.3 for the whole route. These values take some account of a debate about the value of time savings when one can work on the train. So the theoretical benefits are estimated to be worth about twice the costs of construction. However, this economic case largely reflects estimates of the benefits of speedier journeys to business travellers, whose time is supposed to be much more valuable than that of leisure travellers or commuters. And of course the value of this benefit depends on the future number of travellers, which is subject to considerable uncertainty.

What the conventional economic case does not illuminate are the benefits to the cities of the Midlands and the North of the new rail route as the result of new urban developments in those cities. This case has nothing to say about the distribution of benefits other than to different classes of travellers (business, commuters, leisure): nothing about spatial distribution between cities and regions, nor about benefits to existing and future land and property owners. Accordingly, we need an approach to the economic analysis of transport investment that recognizes these consequences, based on the discipline of 'spatial economics', as I shall outline later.

Whatever economic framework is employed, appraising the development potential in the cities to the north of London that would result from HS2 is difficult, given the many uncertainties. Much depends on the efforts made by the city authorities to take advantage of the new rail route – efforts that are seemingly being undertaken with some enthusiasm – as well as on the commercial judgement of developers. It is clear that there is a substantial range of uncertainty associated with such a large, single, hopefully transformational investment. Unless the benefit-to-cost ratio is large, therefore (unlikely for HS2, however it is valued), the political judgement on whether to proceed could not be based on a clear economic case. We cannot be sure that the main beneficiaries of HS2 will not be businesses based in London. The challenge for the cities to the north is to foil this outcome.

In contrast to HS2, Crossrail, the new 100 kilometre east–west rail route through London – currently under construction at a cost of £15 billion and due to open in 2018 – is relatively uncontroversial. It will add 10 per cent to London's rail capacity, supporting economic and population growth, and linking Heathrow to Canary Wharf, where the number of people presently employed (100,000) is likely to double. Although the economic case for this investment focused on travel time savings and disregarded the expected value of real estate development, the real-world benefit is development: to grow London's economy and to house its expanding population. Also apparent is a big boost to the values of existing properties along the route: a windfall gain to property owners. There is a serious mismatch between the notional economic benefits and the real, predictable and observable business case benefits.

89

A similar business case will apply to Crossrail 2: a planned route through London from the suburbs in the south-west to those in the north-east. This will run through the Upper Lea Valley, an area of former industrial land with scope for substantial housing development when made more accessible to employment opportunities in central London. Again, the disconnect is stark between the conventional economic case based on time saving and the business case based on economic development and population growth.

One transport investment where the relationship to property development is particularly strong is the extension of the Northern Line by two stops to Nine Elms and the disused Battersea Power Station: a London landmark just up the river from the Houses of Parliament. This new rail link unlocks brownfield land for the development of commercial and residential river-front properties. A range of transport options was considered, and that adopted was the most expensive, costing £1 billion, justified by the high value of the property development. The developers are contributing about a quarter of this directly, and the government has agreed to earmark the increase in business property taxes (business rates) arising from the development to cover the remainder.

It is noteworthy that developers of such high-value property in London see it as essential to have a nearby Underground link, as opposed to improved roads for the limousines of the residents. More generally, many medium-priced new apartments in inner suburbs with good public transport links are constructed with no available car parking, neither internal nor permitted in regulated street spaces. This does not seem to inhibit sales.

The Northern Line extension highlights the scope for getting developers to contribute directly to the financing of transport investments. In many other situations, however, the increase in property values may be too modest to justify a developer's cash contribution to the transport improvement. For instance, making possible new (if more downmarket) housing development is a feature of the case for extending London's Bakerloo Line from Elephant and Castle to Lewisham. Of the two routes under consideration, the preferred one, through a less salubrious area, offers more opportunities for housing development than the alternative, which runs through a district that is already gentrified.

However, where transport investments result in a substantial uplift of real estate values, there is a strong case for that benefit being shared between the property developer and the transport authority through a routinely applicable mechanism. Transport for London is in conversation with the Treasury about how to invest in infrastructure using devolved business rates, and is arguing that a proportion of stamp duty (a national tax on property sales) should be allocated to pay for transport to new housing developments.

Governance

These London rail investment projects are contributing to the marked shift away from car use in the city that I discussed in chapter 4. They also fit within a considered, articulated strategy for the city's development, unique in Britain. The present governance for London, established in 2000, comprises an elected mayor plus a small assembly of elected members. The mayor is responsible for the transport system and for strategic planning, while the individual London boroughs are responsible for education, social services and other local matters.

An important development in London's strategic planning was the Infrastructure Plan 2050, which was issued for consultation in 2014. This addressed the implications of the city's current rapid population growth (London currently has a population of 8.6 million and is projected to reach 11.3 million by 2050 on the central case) with a corresponding growth in employment. With the highest-value employment growth expected in central areas and the main scope for housing growth further out, the strategic case for investment in transport infrastructure is straightforward. The rail schemes discussed above fit into the strategy for growth.

One other important development is the agreement between the Department for Transport and the mayor that Transport for London should become responsible for suburban rail services in south-east

London. This follows naturally from the success of Transport for London in regenerating a number of linked but neglected rail routes to form an inner orbital line known as the Overground. Since it was opened in 2007, passenger numbers have more than tripled as users have taken advantage of its modern high-frequency service, in particular to access more distant yet affordable housing opportunities.

River crossings

While London is, in general, planning sensibly for growth and for investments in its transport system, I am not entirely uncritical. One proposal that is problematic is for two additional river crossings in east London: between the Blackwall Tunnel, to the east of Tower Bridge, and the Dartford Crossing on the M25 orbital motorway. Consultation is underway on new crossings, whether bridge or tunnel, at Gallions Reach near City Airport and further downriver at Belvedere. These river crossings involve building additional road capacity. This is retrograde in that it runs counter to the general direction of transport policy in London in recent years, which has been to invest in additional rail services but not in road capacity. The result has been a steady shift away from car use at the same time as London has thrived economically, culturally and socially.

There is an inherent problem with river crossings in east London: the width of the river. If this were as narrow as it is in west London, then many more bridges would be possible. On the other hand, if the Thames were twice as wide as it is, then intermediate crossings at Gallions Reach and Belvedere would be ruled out on cost grounds. Given the actual width of the river, a couple of extra crossings are feasible, albeit at a cost of around £1 billion each, but even with these additions, there would still be substantial constraints on cross-river traffic.

The proposals for new river crossings raise two related questions: whether the additional road traffic that would result is likely to be so great as to cause significant additional congestion on the road network, and whether the numbers of users would be sufficiently high to foster a worthwhile amount of development. Transport for London has issued a report on the traffic impact of new crossings, based on a demand model. The assumption is that use of the new crossings will be charged, with tolls set at the rate for the Dartford crossing (£2.50 for a car at peak times). The findings of the traffic modelling are quite complex but generally indicate reduced congestion while overall flows across all crossings are little changed. This is because the model does not allow for any land use changes that could occur as a result of changes in accessibility. However, the hoped-for development as a result of the new crossings would depend on land use changes: new homes and new places of employment. The modelling therefore underestimates the likely growth of traffic and provides limited insight into the congestion consequences.

We know from the National Travel Survey that average travel time remains unchanged in the long run at close to an hour a day. This means that investments that increase speed of travel result in people making longer trips to access more opportunities and choices, which in turn results in changed land use and enhanced land and property values, reflecting the greater access. So we may expect that if new river crossings are built, they will fill with traffic to the point where congestion inhibits further growth: the basis of the maxim that you cannot build your way out of congestion. The benefit will be seen as development of land and property, which is what is desired.

How much development may we expect from additional river crossings? The proposal is that these will have one general traffic lane and one lane for buses and heavy goods vehicles, in each direction. So the scope for growth of commuting seems limited. A further constraining factor is the tolls assumed, both to help finance the new crossings and to manage demand. At £2.50 per car per traverse, this adds £25 to a regular weekly car commute, on top of the usual running costs (£34 a week on average for all households), which could be enough to deter many drivers who are not accustomed to paying tolls for travelling to work.

A study commissioned from consultants has identified property market areas in east London and how these might benefit from additional cross-river connectivity by road. It was concluded that there is over twice as much floor space capacity that could support employment on the north side of the river as on the south side, with the majority of this difference in the office sector. This potential imbalance in employment growth, combined with a relatively even distribution of potential housing growth, would lead to a greater demand for trips from those on the south side of the river commuting to the north. The study estimated that the two proposed crossings would result in a gross impact of around 20,000 additional homes and 400,000 square metres of commercial floor space. This increase is modest – less than 10 per cent of total potential development across the wider area – and prompts the question of whether building new river crossings represents the best value for money in improving connectivity and stimulating development.

There would also be an opportunity cost for new river crossings: what could be achieved spending the money in another way. Arguably, new and improved radial rail routes from east and south-east London would be likely to stimulate more development, both housing and commercial, taking advantage of lower land costs beyond central London. This would be consistent with the consultants' observation that while demand for housing in east London is strong, only sites with good links to the

employment centres of central London are being proposed as sites for development.

Spatial planning

Notwithstanding this river crossings issue, London
offers a good model for the effective planning and operation of the transport system for a major city region.
Other cities are beginning to follow London's lead:
progress made possible by the willingness of the present government to devolve powers to cities prepared
to have elected mayors. Manchester is in the lead, with
the creation of Transport for Greater Manchester in
2011. Beyond the individual cities, there is the 'Northern
Powerhouse': a proposal by George Osborne, Chancellor of the Exchequer, to boost economic growth in the
North of England, particularly in the core cities of Liverpool, Manchester, Leeds, Sheffield and Newcastle. The
aim is to use transport investment to achieve additional
urban agglomeration benefits and so to rebalance the
UK economy away from London and the South-East.

The example of London argues for a spatial plan to
provide the context and rationale for transport investment in the northern cities to accommodate population
and economic growth. One possible outcome, perhaps
tacitly, would recognize Manchester as the main centre
of the region, with an emphasis on the development of

that city as a centre for business services. Another idea, perhaps politically more feasible, would be a multicentric region somewhat analogous to the Randstad, the well-connected group of the main Dutch industrial cities, with a mix of manufacturing and services. One key question is how to take advantage of the research potential of the universities, both for the cities in which they are located and across the region. Related to this is the question of where to locate businesses in relation to the availability of skilled staff.

At present there is no mechanism for spatial planning across the northern cities as a group, and hence no consideration of options for the location of population and economic growth across the region. In the absence of a spatial plan, decisions on transport investments will be an important influence on spatial development in ways that need to be addressed as part of the investment case. In London, expected economic and population growth is the main determinant of future transport investment, which is therefore relatively unproblematic in principle. For the northern cities, such growth is less obviously a given, and a desired role for transport investment is to foster growth.

It is not straightforward to develop a persuasive case for specific investments in the context of the northern cities. Estimates of benefits based on travel time savings give no indication of the spatial location or likely scale of development. Estimates of 'wider impacts' depend on either rules of thumb or ambitious modelling that cannot be validated. It is therefore hard to say, based on conventional appraisal methods, how transport investments will benefit the economies of these cities.

It is easier to predict changes in land use arising from transport investments that change travel-to-work patterns. Faster travel may be expected to result in people seeking housing and employment opportunities further afield. This would both improve the efficiency of labour markets and create opportunities for housing development. For rail investments in particular, the location of new housing should be planned as part of the investment case. Urban rail investment can allow cities to grow to higher density while meeting the mobility needs of the population. Regional rail plays a similar role. The tram-train being piloted between Sheffield and Rotherham is an interesting innovation: a tram route that shares track with an existing railway. Bus Rapid Transit – buses on dedicated traffic-free routes – likewise provides speedy, reliable travel but at a cost lower than light rail trams. Higher urban population densities generate agglomeration benefits – not only economic but also cultural and social – that enhance the attractiveness of cities, provided other aspects of urban liveability receive adequate attention. Accordingly, both urban and regional rail investments justify positive consideration.

What is unclear, however, is the extent to which better regional rail links that improve connectivity *between* cities would generate economic benefits over and above those associated with housing and labour markets for individual cities. Glasgow and Edinburgh are well-connected cities but it would be hard to say to what extent this east–west connectivity, as opposed to north–south connectivity, contributes to economic success.

Road investments are even more problematic. For instance, the scheme to enlarge the east–west M62 motorway to four lanes along its entire length is intended to support the northern economy but would induce local commuter use that would limit the benefits to long-distance users. A new road link between Manchester and Sheffield, largely in a tunnel under the Peak District National Park, might be of less use to commuters but would be expensive and hard to justify on the grounds of improved connections between two cities that are already well connected. More generally, road investments intended to improve connectivity between cities within a region, whether north–south or east–west, are likely to be nullified by the induced traffic from local users.

The government, together with the city regions and other local partners, has issued a Northern Transport Strategy, which includes ambitious plans for road construction. However, these seem of very uncertain benefit, albeit more consistent with a multicentric region in which manufacturing remains important. On the other hand, the plans for integrated information and ticketing across all public transport modes, which form part of the overall strategy, are clearly sensible and, as digital applications, may be expected to be far more cost-effective than investment in civil engineering technologies. Predictive journey time information on the road network would be another worthwhile innovation.

Politicians and advisors

Government interest in transport has fluctuated considerably over the years. For much of the past half century, the Department for Transport has not ranked high in status amongst Whitehall ministries, the Secretary of State for Transport of the day being either on their way up or on their way out of the Cabinet, and generally keeping a low profile. But at other times there has been more interest and bigger investment plans, as is the case currently. George Osborne is keen to invest in infrastructure, even in a period of general austerity. Andrew Adonis, Labour Secretary of State for Transport 2009–10, and another politician who is enthusiastic about transport investment, is a strong advocate of HS2 and the east London river crossings.

Political leadership can be valuable in getting things done. But there is a problem if the public commitment to a big investment comes before the analysis. The professional civil servants responsible for the economic appraisal of proposed investments are conflicted. They need to do a good professional job but also meet the political needs of their minister. The upshot can be a somewhat tendentious analysis in which judgement is exercised in a way that attempts to reconcile the professional and political objectives.

This is not ideal: it would be better to do the analysis of the full range of options first and then make a political judgement about the preferred possibilities. This is what has happened with the thorny problem of airport capacity in south-east England, where the independent experts comprising the Airports Commission narrowed down a wide range of possibilities to three for detailed analysis, eventually recommending another runway at Heathrow, as discussed in chapter 5. However, the usefulness of such an approach depends on the validity of the analysis. In the case of air travel, I pointed out the failure to consider the way the market might develop if no new runway were to be built. For surface travel, the problem is the shortcomings of economic appraisal focused on notional time savings.

The government recently established a National Infrastructure Commission, an independent body whose purpose is to identify the UK's strategic infrastructure needs over the next 10–30 years and propose solutions to the most pressing infrastructure issues. The Commission's initial remit from the government included transport investment both in the north of

England and in London. The chair is Andrew Adonis and one of the Commission's members is Lord Heseltine, the former deputy prime minister who has long championed the regeneration of Britain's inner cities through infrastructure investment. Another Commission member is Demis Hassabis, artificial intelligence researcher and head of DeepMind Technologies, a company acquired by Google for a reported £400 million. He may be an advocate for twenty-first-century digital infrastructure rather than yet more twentieth-century concrete and tarmac.

The National Infrastructure Commission has the potential to improve decision-making by ensuring that sound analysis takes place in advance of decisions. The interesting question is how the Commission will function. Will it be a cheerleader for those keen to undertake big civil engineering projects with other people's money? Or will it be a critical friend to government departments and local authorities needing to get best value from constrained budgets? Initial signs are mixed.

The Commission's uncontentious endorsement of Crossrail 2 recognized the inadequacy of conventional economic analysis (which does not take account of changes in land use) for a project that has the potential to facilitate the development of 200,000 new homes by improving transport connectivity. The Commission also advocated strengthening the east–west rail network in the north of England, designated 'HS3', and particularly the TransPennine route between Manchester and Leeds, the two largest cities in the region.

However, the Commission's recommendations for roads investment were not persuasively argued. While the use of the motorway system by commuters was recognized, there was no analysis of how enlargement of the road network would impact on different classes of road user: commuters, long-distance car traffic and road freight. The economic consequences would be quite different if the main gainers were car-based commuters to the nearest city, as opposed to intercity business travellers and freight traffic.

There are two useful models for how independent bodies can advise government. The Office for Budget Responsibility was created to provide independent and authoritative analysis of the UK's public finances. The Committee on Climate Change has the tasks of advising the government on emissions targets and reporting to parliament on progress made in reducing greenhouse gas emissions and preparing for climate change. Both of these bodies are seen to be independent and their advice carries weight on that account.

It will be important for the National Infrastructure Commission to look critically at the analytical methodologies currently employed by government departments, to ensure these are fit for purpose. I have laboured the shortcomings of transport modelling and economic appraisal. One general issue is the lack of sufficient attention given to the 'do-minimum' case: what happens if an investment is not made.

In most areas of life there is a 'bias for action'. Professionals and businesses earn income if investments are made, which is why they are prone to giving the advice: 'just do it' – especially when it is other people's money that is being spent. However, there is extensive evidence, particularly from the financial sector, of wasteful expenditure: in mergers and acquisitions, and in active fund management compared with passive, for instance. For transport investment, thinking through the consequences of not investing is important, but it is not easy. The decision made in the 1970s not to rebuild London's road network to accommodate the expected growth in car use turned out to be sound, as judged by the subsequent success of the city.

The proposal to build a third runway at Heathrow is a current difficult issue, given the environmental impacts and questions about financing through higher airport charges. The economic analysis that supported construction paid too little attention to the 'do-minimum' case, in which a capacity constraint persists but the very competitive market for air travel responds by prioritizing business travellers at this hub airport. As with road capacity in London, an airport capacity constraint is far less likely to detract from the success of the city than proponents of new capacity suppose. We should therefore be relaxed about constructing another runway at Heathrow: if it is too difficult to do so politically, we could manage without.

We need a National Infrastructure Commission that can prioritize investments by recognizing the occasions when it is better not to build additional infrastructure, not least to free resources where this can make a real difference to the economic rebalancing of Britain in favour of regions beyond London and the south-east of England. Spatial and economic planning are currently out of fashion, whereas infrastructure planning is in. We need the Commission to recognize the bigger picture and make best use of the substantial available funds.

One important issue is the government's Road Investment Strategy 2015–2020, which commits £15 billion to be invested in over 100 major schemes on the Strategic Road Network, including over 1,300 miles of extra lanes. This expenditure package contains a number of ring-fenced funds for particular purposes, such as reducing environmental impacts (£300 million), improving air quality (£100 million), investing in innovative technologies (£150 million) and supporting growth in employment and housing (£100 million). These specific funds reflect worthwhile objectives but are ring-fenced, presumably because the economic case for the investments seems weak, compared with road construction, which comprises around 95 per cent of the total and which would be assessed as offering good value for money on the standard approach to economic appraisal. My contention is that an analytical framework that reflected reality would yield a very different balance: much more expenditure on innovative digital technologies and in support of employment and housing growth, and much less on new road construction, vainly intended to relieve congestion.

The National Infrastructure Commission's latest task (as of June 2016) is to make recommendations for investment along the Cambridge–Milton Keynes–Oxford corridor to yield a single knowledge-intensive cluster with the greatest economic development potential and with the necessary homes and jobs. It is noteworthy that this remit is solely from the Chancellor of the Exchequer and not jointly with the Secretary of State for Transport, as past precedent would suggest, perhaps reflecting the lack of an analytical framework for relating transport investment to development, employment and housing.

Smarter travel

The National Infrastructure Commission is concerned with big investments. But we should not overlook the value of small-scale improvements to the transport system. Indeed, an approach developed in recent years, called variously 'smarter choices' or 'smarter travel', aims to get people out of their cars by promoting walking and cycling, the 'slow modes', as well as public transport, all through relatively low-cost schemes. The aims are to enhance sustainability and improve health through more exercise. As well as investment in infrastructure, e.g. cycle lanes, effort is being put into changing people's behaviour via marketing and promotion techniques. Evaluation of such initiatives indicates that typically 10 per cent of those targeted change their behaviour and make less use of their cars.

A constraint on getting people to switch from cars to other modes of transport is that these would generally be slower, and would therefore reduce access and choice. Accordingly, people who do switch are likely to be those making unaccompanied shorter trips. A constraint on enhancing sustainability is the likelihood that the road space freed up by those switching to other modes will be taken advantage of by other motorists to make longer trips on account of the higher speeds that are possible. Accordingly, it is recognized that the benefits of reduced car use by smarter travel interventions would need to be 'locked in' by means of measures that prevent other motorists driving more – by allocating more carriageway to cyclists and pedestrians, for instance. So 'hard measures' are needed to lock in the benefits from 'soft measures'. But the question is then: which have the greatest effect? The hard measures that cannot be avoided or the soft measures involving persuasion? The substantial shift away from car use in London described in chapter 4 is to a great extent the result of road capacity constraints, with the persuasive approaches playing a minor role at best.

There is a good deal of enthusiasm for smarter travel measures among younger transport professionals working for local authorities, who actively bid for funds that the Department for Transport makes available on a competitive basis to support walking, cycling and public transport use. They would like to get people out of their cars and onto their bikes. But we need clear thinking about what can be achieved.

We know that the level of urban cycling is high in countries such as the Netherlands and Denmark, and in some cities like Oxford. Cycling is growing in popularity as a leisure activity: for fit male professionals, cycling is the new golf. However, the evidence is that the growth of daily cycle use is mainly due to people switching from public transport, with another factor being existing cyclists making more trips on improved routes. In the Netherlands around a quarter of all trips are made by bike, compared with 2 per cent in Britain, but the share of public transport trips is half that in the UK.

Do we want to get people off public transport and onto bicycles? This can be helpful in a city like London, with a rapidly growing population and crowding on pub-lic transport. Crowding builds up on radial commuter bus and rail routes as the city centre is approached. Invest-ment in cycling facilities can relieve this overcrowding on the final few miles and may allow costly investment in public transport to be delayed or even avoided, which could be the main economic benefits of such investment. Boris Johnson, London's mayor from 2008 to 2016, was a keen cyclist who promoted ambitious plans for 'Cycling Superhighways', aimed at encouraging nervous cyclists by segregating them from general traffic. Cycle use in London during the morning rush hour has more than trebled since 2000: an indicator of the success of cycling promotion measures that go with the grain of concerns about physical fitness and the need to exercise.

While promotion of cycling has a clear purpose in big cities with crowded public transport, the benefits are less clear in smaller cities and towns, where bus use has been declining. A big difference has developed between bus use in London and in the rest of England. Margaret Thatcher's government deregulated and privatized local bus services outside of London in the 1980s, the main aim being to get benefits from on-road competition between bus companies, but in the event this rarely occurred. Passenger demand for bus services in England outside of London fell almost continuously from the time of deregulation to the mid 2000s. Exceptions to the general rule of decline have been found in free-standing towns – such as Brighton, Oxford, Reading and Nottingham – that have clear governance and long-term stable policies to support buses, with both formal partnership agreements and practical collaborations based on trust and good personal relationships.

In contrast, Transport for London retained overall responsibility for bus services as an integrated network, albeit with operation of buses on individual routes being franchised to private companies who tendered for the contracts competitively. Bus passenger numbers in London have grown steadily over the period in which numbers in the rest of England have fallen, which points to the advantages of an integrated network with easy payments using the popular Oyster card, online time-tables and real-time indicators at bus stops.

The success of buses in London has led to the govern-ment allowing other major cities with devolved powers over transport to adopt a similar franchise model if they wish. New legislation is planned that will allow local councils more freedom to run their own bus services, to facilitate Oyster-style ticketing across the country, and to create new bus travel apps as bus companies are made to share more details about services.

Road pricing

Another reason for the success of buses in London has been the scale of investment in modern vehicles, in bus priority lanes and in digital infrastructure. One source of funding is the congestion charge levied on vehicles entering a central zone during working hours. This was a brave innovation of London's first mayor, Ken

Livingstone, a politician on the left who adopted the approach to rationing a scarce resource (urban road space) by price that is often endorsed by economists, particularly those on the political right.

Generally, politicians shy away from road pricing, anticipating public resistance, as indeed has manifested when particular proposals were subject to local referenda in Manchester and Edinburgh. The economists bemoan a lack of political will, but arguably they should recognize the preference of the public for the shared experience of traffic congestion to the perceived lack of fairness of allowing the better off to pay for faster travel. Generally, transport is a relatively egalitarian domain, in that it is usually difficult to travel faster by paying more. First class travel on trains and planes offers greater comfort, not greater speed (although a more costly direct long-haul flight will take less time than a cheaper flight via an intermediate hub). On the roads, subject to legal speed limits and traffic congestion, the reasonably priced family car will progress just as well as the top-of-the-range coupé.

The congestion charging zone in London has been successful in that it has worked technically, it is accepted by Londoners, and it has generated funds for investment in the transport system. When introduced in 2003, there was a useful reduction in congestion and an increase in traffic speeds, which then dissipated as freed-up road space was reallocated to other modes of transport – particularly buses and bicycles – as well as to better-quality public space. As a result, congestion in central London is now no better than when the charge was introduced.

Towards the end of his term of office, Ken Livingstone extended congestion charging to a new zone to the west of the original zone. His successor, Boris Johnson, withdrew charging from this western extension. The impact on traffic of the extension and its subsequent withdrawal was pretty small, suggesting that congestion charging is not as important in regulating demand for car travel as economists have supposed. What is probably more important are the constraints imposed by parking controls and charges: an approach that can be adjusted incrementally, as opposed to the all-or-nothing of congestion charging.

Road pricing is attractive to economists but not to politicians unless they are particularly brave or head a finance ministry. Taxation on petrol and diesel fuel for road vehicles is a major source of revenue for governments, particularly in Britain, where such taxes are relatively high. However, this source will decline over time on account of both improved fuel efficiency, arising from regulations prompted by concerns about climate change and polluting emissions, and a progressive switch to electric propulsion. Treasury ministers will therefore become increasingly interested in road pricing as a means of raising revenue, not least to cover the costs of road maintenance and construction.

The development of digital infrastructure to support the transport system may offer an opportunity for the introduction of road pricing as part of a package of services to both assist and charge road users. Two-thirds of people in Britain currently own a smartphone, a proportion that is rapidly rising. It would therefore be possible in the fairly near future to require all vehicle users to have a smartphone, which would allow their use of the road network to be tracked, as indeed happens now with many popular apps for route finding (with privacy respected, as at present). Collaboration between the road authorities, the phone companies and the app providers would allow road users to be offered choices over time and route in which charging was one element: for instance, the fastest route at a higher charge, a slower route at a lower charge, a scenic route, or a free route at a time when traffic levels were low. As well as offering benefits in terms of journey time reliability to individuals, road users as a whole would benefit from the more efficient use of the network.

Decisions and models

Digital technologies, which benefit from fast innovation cycles and economies of scale, will generally be far more cost-effective than civil engineering technologies. Moving earth, pouring concrete and rolling tarmac are costly and don't help deal with road congestion – a fact we have long recognized in cities and which we once recognized, but have recently seemed to forget, as being true for roads between cities too. The current enthusiasm for investing in infrastructure needs to be refocused on the potential impact of digital infrastructure in sweating the historic assets of the transport system.

For sensible decisions to be made about investment, we need a framework for decision-making that is fit for purpose. The current long-established methodologies are obsolete and misleading. Conventional economic appraisal of transport investment proposals focuses on time savings, but these are short term, not long term. The long-term impact of such investments is to make land more accessible, which prompts development, but the enhanced value of land and property is not counted in conventional appraisal. The economic case for an investment is therefore unrelated to the business case. Moreover, conventional economic appraisal is weak in accounting for improved reliability, which is the main benefit of digital technologies. The present framework results in serious biases in decision-making: too much investment in civil engineering technologies on inter-urban roads; too little investment in digital technologies; and too little investment in urban rail because the enhanced value of land and property is not recognized.

The conventional approach to economic analysis is concerned with benefits to users of the transport system – benefits that are aggregated across all future users to estimate the total economic value, which is then compared with the costs of the investment to reach a decision on value for money. This can be appropriate when the focus is on users, e.g. if we are assessing the value of a subsidy to sustain a bus service. However, politicians are currently concerned, not unreasonably, with how and where transport investment can foster economic growth. In this context, the relationship between user benefits and economic development is very tenuous. What is needed is a more direct approach, based on the established discipline of 'spatial economics'.

Spatial economics was founded by the nineteenth-century German economist Johann Heinrich von Thünen, who considered the relationship between the rents that farmers could afford to pay to landowners and the value of their produce when sold in the market in the nearest city. The further the land was from the city, the higher the transport costs and, consequently, the less the rent that could be afforded, all else equal. Land sufficiently far from the city could not yield any produce that could be sold at a profit after transport costs. Von Thünen published his seminal work a decade or two before the coming of the railways, which effected a sharp reduction in transport costs and so made vast swathes of land newly available for agricultural production.

This approach to economic analysis recognizes a direct relationship between land use, land value and transport costs. It was subsequently extended to urban areas, where the greater the distance of housing from the central business district, the greater the transport costs and the lower house prices and rents. Reducing transport costs through the use of new technology allows additional useful space for habitation. This is the basis of 'urban economics' and, more generally, of 'economic geography' and 'location theory'. Given that the purpose of transport is to move people and goods through space, it is remarkable that spatial economic thinking is so infrequently applied to decision-making. One reason is that transport economists and allied specialists have grown comfortable with a framework that excludes the additional complexities of changes in land use.

Some effort has been devoted to developing models in which land use and transport are jointly modelled, but these are generally seen as complex and expensive to run. And because they have not been required for conventional appraisal, there has been little support for their further development. Nevertheless, there is scope for their wider use. I mentioned earlier the river-front development linked to extension of London's Northern Line, where a number of alternative transport investments were considered. This implies that the combined land use and transport options were jointly modelled, prior to a decision being made about the preferred option. I also mentioned the debate about the proposed east London river crossings, where there has been a study of the property development expected to result. Again, a model of the relationship between land use change and transport investment is implied.

So I believe there is considerable scope for improving how we model the consequences of transport investment as a basis for making decisions. The main need is to base models of future behaviour on open-minded evaluation of the outcomes of similar past investments: an evidence-based approach. By 'open-minded' I mean that we should look thoroughly at all actual outcomes, free of preconceptions about what we wanted or expected to happen. In particular, we should count time savings only when these are observed in practice, and we should fully recognize changes in land use and values where these are observed in the market. An evidenced-based approach avoids the problem of double counting benefits since people can only do one thing at a time. If they take the benefit of an improvement to the transport system that allows faster travel by travelling further, then there are no time savings to be used for more work or leisure; and vice versa.

Models in the physical sciences aim to describe the state of some part of the universe in precise mathematical terms. A better model displaces an earlier model because of improved accounting for observations made, whether through radio telescopes or particle colliders. The world of the social sciences is very complicated, however, so economic models can only aim to account for some aspects of what is observed. The challenge for economic analysis is to decide which of a number of possible models is most appropriate to illuminate the decision in question.

The transport models that support the conventional approach to economic appraisal are not best suited to supporting decision-making where the aim is to invest to stimulate economic growth, which necessarily involves changes in land use. Instead, we need to develop models that incorporate land use and appraisal techniques, both based on the principles of spatial economics. Transport models should be constrained to hold average travel time constant in the long run, consistent with the evidence of the National Travel Survey.

The policy aim of stimulating economic growth is quite high level. A second high-level aim of transport investment is to accommodate population growth, which is quite rapid in Britain at present: another 10 million inhabitants are expected by 2040. However, as well as facilitating these strategic aims, transport investments need to meet the requirements of specific locations. The question that must be asked is: what kind of a place do we wish to live in?

How do we want to live?

One model that we increasingly understand, and which has many attractions, is the big city, exemplified by London, as outlined in chapter 4. People are attracted by the bright lights and the good jobs to work, study and live, particularly in the formative years. Success attracts those aspiring to success. The economics of agglomeration improve the productivity of businesses, with analogous cultural and social benefits. Growth in the service sector in developed economies is increasingly located in central urban areas. The entertainment and hospitality sectors follow their clients, collocating with workplaces. Population density increases. More people means more demand for public transport, more investment in more frequent services, which attract more patronage and revenue: a virtuous circle. Car use declines and sustainability improves. New urban rail routes make brownfield land accessible for development, both in inner areas such as Docklands and in outer areas of former industrial use. Increasing the capacity of existing rail lines allows population growth in existing neighbourhoods through infill building, higher-density use of existing properties and, potentially, redevelopment of low-density suburbs.

We find it very difficult to build sufficient new homes to meet demand in much of Britain, with the result that house prices are rising rapidly, to such an extent that to many younger people the prospect of owning their own home seems increasingly distant. However, most home purchases are of existing properties, so one approach to relieving pressure in the housing market is to improve the efficiency of use of existing properties. The older couple whose children have left home, 'empty-nesters', might be inclined to downsize in order to release funds to supplement pensions. But the choice of suitable homes for those in later life is limited – this is not something we are good at building in Britain. However, a new or improved rail service to serve the neighbourhood would feed through into higher property prices, increasing the incentive to move, thereby freeing up a family house for a couple with a young family. Rail investment can stimulate churn of existing properties, thus helping to relieve pressure in the housing market.

The big city model for living has many attractions. But this lifestyle, whether in the inner city or the outer suburbs, is not for everyone. What are the alternatives for smaller cities and larger towns? There seem to be two main choices. They could attempt to emulate the big city, but on a smaller scale, promoting a sense of place around an attractive historic city centre or a substantially new one. This would involve pushing back the car to allow interactions between people that make for the vibrant life of the city. As well as the stick of parking controls, they would need the carrot of speedy reliable public transport: something better than the usual bus – perhaps a revived old rail route, a tram or Bus Rapid

Transit. In Britain, we tend to think that trams cannot be economically justified in small cities. But thirty French cities, some quite small, have tram systems, mostly built in recent decades.

The alternative approach, now rather traditional, is to attempt to accommodate the car. This approach is in part driven by the anxiety that car users would take their trade to nearby towns if such accommodation were less convenient. Such cities may be active in promoting smarter travel measures, but these are unlikely to make much impact on car use. There is a degree of conflict between cars and people that is hard to avoid. If cars are accommodated, there is severance between neighbourhoods and diminished social and informal business interactions between people.

For many cities, one possible option would be to adapt to the needs of an ageing population, aiming to take advantage of the spending power of the growing numbers of people in later life. This cohort is particularly heterogeneous with respect to health, wealth, life stage and lifestyle, such that chronological age is only a limited indicator of status and need. In general, people in later life wish to retain their mobility and retain access to desired destinations as much as possible, and will want substitutes when a preferred means of travel is no longer practicable, in particular when driving has to be abandoned. So there is a need to facilitate the transitions of later life and mitigate their adverse consequences, which include loss of mobility, reduced access to services, iso-lation and loneliness. The World Health Organization's concept of 'age-friendly cities' is a helpful approach, as is the concept of 'inclusive design', the maxim of which is: 'design for the young and you exclude the old, design for the old and you include the young'. So an age-friendly city is also a 'people-friendly city' – all a bit motherhood-and-apple-pie, perhaps, but none the worse for that.

There is a great diversity of towns and cities in Britain, all of which grapple with traffic using varying approaches and with varying degrees of success. The government is attempting to stimulate innovation by devolving power to cities that are judged able to cope. It also attempts to foster innovative transport initiatives by means of competition for funding programmes, but this tends to lead to opportunistic bids that lack a strategic context. So what should be done? I set out my views in the final chapter that follows.

Chapter 8

A manifesto for an intelligent transport policy

In this final chapter I summarize the principles that should guide us in making decisions about investment in transport. Christian Wolmar, in his book in this Perspectives series, argued that there has never been a coherent transport policy in this country. I attempt to respond to his challenge by outlining one.

The transport system is mainly a means to an end. More and better transport allows us access to more opportunities and choices. But those opportunities and choices depend on the destination. A road to nowhere is of little use. So transport investment has to be seen as part of the broad pattern of public and private investment by which we try to improve our society. Here are the key principles.

The need to plan for economic development

The central message of this book is that any investment that increases the speed of travel will allow people to spread further across the landscape. The case for any particular investment should centre on whether the dispersal is desirable or not. The benefits of improved access and connectivity may be offset by undesirable consequences such as more traffic congestion, noise and emissions.

More and further travel changes how land is used so *the local planning authority, the developer and the transport authority should plan transport investments jointly.* This ensures that the economic benefits of the transport investment are locked in. Transport investments that disregard the consequential changes in land use (and hence economic development) are speculative. Some succeed, and sometimes brilliantly, as with the initial phase of the Docklands Light Railway that stimulated the development of Canary Wharf. Other speculative investments disappoint: the Humber Bridge, for example, which is a splendid civil engineering achievement but is underused.

Transport investment needs to be an integral part of investment for economic development. The economy can benefit from transport investment that makes land more accessible for development of housing and of commercial and industrial premises.

However, although transport investment is essentially government led, whether by national government or by local authorities, general economic development, including of land and property, is largely led by the private sector. For more than a generation, governments in Britain have been reluctant to play an active role in economic development, which is often seen as the risky business of 'picking winners'.

More surprisingly, national government has proved reluctant to plan for population growth, which is currently quite rapid in Britain. London as a city-region is actively planning for population and employment growth, and for the transport investment needed to link homes with jobs. Other city-regions acquiring devolved powers will follow suit. But for England as a whole there is a policy gap. The 2012 National Planning Policy Framework exercise should have addressed population growth, but the opportunity was missed.

So we have substantial planned national public investment in roads and railways that is not linked to expected or hoped-for economic and population growth. The odds are that we will get ineffective transport expenditure with damaging environmental consequences. *The government needs to be willing to plan for future development.*

Planning for economic and population growth could be incorporated within planning for transport investment, recognizing that the latter is in fashion politically whereas the former are not. This approach would be natural for local authorities operating at city-region scale or above. It may also be possible for the National Infrastructure Commission, thinking regionally and nationally, and therefore tacitly acting as a National Planning Commission.

A new approach to assessing transport investment

If we are to have an approach to transport investment that delivers the economic and social results we want, then a valid analytical framework to aid decision makers is essential. At present, the analytical framework is not fit for purpose.

Whatever the planning context, there are two common-sense principles we should adopt for decisions on transport investment: base such decisions on the evidence gained from the outcome of previous investments; and address transport investment not in isolation but as part of wider investment for growth.

An evidence-based approach to transport investment ought not to be contentious. However, the conventional transport economist approach is theory based, not evidence based. Their theory is that the value of transport investments can be estimated by calculating the total time supposedly saved by faster travel. But these time savings are not real. What is real and readily observed are the changes in how land is used and valued when transport investment makes such land more accessible – which the economists disregard.

We need to value proposed transport investments on the basis of the real changes that will be brought about.

This requires a holistic analysis of all the related investments that will be made, by both the private sector and the public sector. Such an approach is gaining support, particularly in London where employment and housing development is increasingly seen as the main rationale for planned investments such as Crossrail 2.

Having the wrong conceptual framework is not just a theoretical shortcoming. Mistaken investments are costing many billions of pounds of public expenditure (but not of private expenditure: firms are rightly realistic when committing shareholders' money). We invest too little in urban rail schemes because we do not take proper account of the economic benefits of higher-density cities. We are investing too much in civil engineering technologies on inter-urban roads in the vain hope of building our way out of congestion. And we are neglecting investment in digital technologies, which will be the most cost-effective way of tackling the problem of traffic congestion.

We need to reconsider the tools used to forecast the future. It is not sensible to simplify transport models by omitting changes in land use that result from transport investment, because changes in land use invariably result from transport investment. We also need to recognize important changes in travel behaviour such as the peak car phenomenon, and the attractions for the young of urban living without a car, as well as emerging evidence of market maturity in air travel.

A holistic approach

The route to an intelligent transport policy must start with *an analytical framework that focuses on how investment can meet economic and societal objectives.* Such a framework allows comparison of different kinds of transport investment, e.g. rail versus road for a particular intercity link. It also informs debate about regional allocations of national expenditure.

For example, investment in walking and cycling is usually modest in cost and good for the health of the population: benefits rightly taken into account in cost–benefit analysis from a national perspective. Increased cycling can relieve crowding on public transport, as in London, which is a substantial economic benefit if public transport investment can be deferred. And to the extent that investment in the 'slow modes' gets people out of their cars for short trips, the quality of town and city centres is enhanced.

The precise investment pattern derived from the principles and policies of an intelligent transport policy will in general emerge from application of the analytical framework to everyday budget allocations for capital expenditure. However, when it comes to large proposed expenditures, such as HS2 or a third runway at Heathrow, the problem is that such projects are not incremental. The environmental consequences are substantial and prompt vocal opposition from those most affected. Any form of economic analysis is problematic, given the major uncertainties about impact. *Decisions on large projects are inevitably subject to more political judgment and need to be treated as special cases*, particularly as regards the justification for such a substantial commitment of national resources.

One aspect of decision-making that requires more attention is to *think through the implications of not making a large investment*. The decision in the 1970s not to build major urban motorways in London turned out to be well judged as the city has thrived as car use has stabilized. More generally, there is a 'bias to action' on the part of consultants and construction firms, and also very often on the part of politicians happy to spend other people's money. This goes along with 'optimism bias', which can lead to hopeful forecasts of both travel demand and construction costs. A careful analysis of the market response to a transport capacity constraint should therefore form part of any decision-making for transport investment of any scale, and particularly for big projects.

How much investment in transport?

The right analytical framework helps decision makers prioritize investments. But how is the overall transport investment budget to be set? Britain is densely settled and has a mature transport system, limiting the scope for cost-effective and environmentally acceptable new infrastructure. The present government has treated transport generously. Capital expenditure by the Department for Transport is due to double, from £6 billion in 2015 to £12 billion in 2020. At present *we need to make better use of this substantial spend, not argue for more.*

Conventional transport economics has reached a dead end. It needs to be absorbed into a spatial economics framework and used to make evidence-based decisions. And conventional travel-demand modelling and forecasting needs to be rethought to include both changes in land use and the changes in behaviour that are taking place as we have transitioned from the twentieth century to the twenty-first. The current political enthusiasm for investment in transport infrastructure is well intentioned but not well thought through. We need better understanding of the benefits, otherwise outcomes will continue to disappoint.

Summary

I summarize the key points of my argument in the following principles.

- Transport investment needs to be an integral part of investment for economic development. The government needs to be willing to plan for future development, for both economic growth and population growth.

- The route to an intelligent transport policy must start from an analytical framework that focuses on how investment can meet economic and societal objectives.

- We need to value proposed transport investments on the basis of the real changes that will be brought about. Holistic analysis of all the related investments that will be made is needed, both by the private sector and by the public sector

- Transport investments should be planned jointly by the local planning authority, developers and the transport authority.

- Decisions on large projects are inevitably subject to more political judgment and need to be treated as special cases. More thought needs to be given to the consequences of *not* making such investments.

- Better use needs to be made of the already substantial planned spending on transport before a case is made for spending to increase.

Sources and further reading

Selected recent published sources for each chapter are shown below, with details given in the subsequent references section for many of the cited works. Web addresses are not cited since they can be cumbersome and can change or disappear. However, current web sources can be found by searching using a few key words from a given title.

The main statistical sources are those of the UK Department for Transport, in particular the National Travel Survey, an annual survey of travel behaviour, Road Traffic Forecasts, and Transport Statistics Great Britain. For London, the annual Travel in London reports are world-leading in their coverage. For international aviation statistics, the Civil Aviation Authority is the key source for passenger numbers; while for visitor numbers, the International Passenger Survey of the Office for National Statistics is the best reference.

The central argument of this book has been developed in a series of my papers published in peer-reviewed journals; these are included in the list of references. Some material is drawn from articles that appear on my own website – www.peakcar.org – where links to my published papers can also be found. Further articles will appear after this book is published. A fuller list of sources can be found in my previous book, *Peak Car: The Future of Travel*, published in 2014.

Chapter 1. An hour a day

For interpretation of National Travel Survey data and four eras of travel, see Metz (2008, 2013a, 2014).

Chapter 2. Space not time

The conventional approach to transport economic analysis can be found in the Department for Transport's web-based Transport Analysis Guidance (WebTAG) and also in standard texts such as Quinet and Vickerman (2004). For thoughtful accounts of current practice and application see the papers by Worsley and Mackie in the list of references below, and also Venables *et al.* (2014). For critiques of the standard approach, see Metz (2008) and Rosewell (2010).

Chapter 3. Peak car

On peak car in the UK, see Le Vine and Jones (2012), Metz (2013a), POST (2013) and Social Research Associates (2015).

On peak car in the US, look for ongoing reports by Michael Sivak of the University of Michigan Transportation Research Institute.

On saturation of demand, see Metz (2010, 2013b).

Chapter 4. Green cities

Future of Cities, a UK government 'Foresight project', has a number of interesting papers, including Metz (2015b). See also Headicar (2015) on urban trends, Metz (2012, 2015a) on travel in London, and Emerson (2014) on traffic in London.

Chapter 5. Up in the air

The reports of the Airports Commission published between 2013 and 2015 are informative. For a critique, see Kay (2015).

Chapter 6. Technologies – slow and fast

There is extensive information available about conventional transport technologies, digital technologies and driverless vehicles from web sources, none of which is definitive. Accessible accounts of urban traffic management and smart ticketing in London are Emerson (2014) and Verma (2014).

Chapter 7. The future of travel

Good critiques of current practice when it comes to fore-casting and modelling are Hartgen (2013) and a paper by Yaron Hollander on his website at CTthink. A useful account of economic modelling generally is Rodrik (2015).

- HS2: The Strategic Case for HS2 (2013); The Economic Case for HS2 (2013); Wolmar (2014).
- Crossrail2: Funding and Financing Study (2014), PricewaterhouseCoopers for Transport for London; Crossrail2: Regional and National Benefits (2015).
- East London river crossings: consultation documents and technical reports issued by Transport for London in 2015.
- National Infrastructure Commission: Transport for a World City (2016); High Speed North (2016).
- 'Northern Powerhouse': Northern Transport Strategy (2015).
- Spatial economics: Quinet and Vickerman (2004).
- Road pricing: Glaister (2014); Johnson et al. (2012).
- Buses: KPMG (2016).
- Devolution: Raikes (2016).
- Changing demography: Metz (2016).

Chapter 8. A manifesto for an intelligent transport policy

An engaging account of transport history and policy can be found in Wolmar (2016).

References

G. Emerson. 2014. Maximising the use of the road network in London. In *Moving Cities: The Future of Urban Travel*, edited by S. Glaister and E. Box. London: RAC Foundation.

S. Glaister. 2014. The Smeed Report at fifty: will road pricing always be ten years away? Smeed Memorial Lecture, Transport Institute, University College London.

D. Hartgen. 2013. Hubris or humility? Accuracy issues for the next 50 years of travel demand modelling. *Transportation* 40:1133–1157.

P. Headicar. 2015. Traffic in towns: the next fifty years. Occasional Paper 6, Independent Transport Commission, London.

P. Johnson, A. Leicester and G. Stoye. 2012. Fuel for thought: the what, why and how of motoring taxation. Institute for Fiscal Studies/RAC Foundation, London.

J. Kay. 2015. No way to plan an airport. *Prospect*, November, pp. 42–44.

KPMG. 2016. Local bus market study. Report to the Department for Transport, KPMG, London.

S. Le Vine and P. Jones. 2012. On the move: making sense of car and train travel trends in Britain. RAC Foundation, London.

P. Mackie and T. Worsley. 2013. International comparisons of transport appraisal practice: overview report. Institute for Transport Studies, University of Leeds.

D. Metz. 2008. The myth of travel times saving. *Transport Reviews* 28(3):321–336.

D. Metz. 2010. Saturation of demand for daily travel. *Transport Reviews* 30(5):659–674.

REFERENCES

D. Metz. 2012. Demographic determinants of daily travel demand. *Transport Policy* 21(1):20–25.

D. Metz. 2013a. Peak car and beyond: the fourth era of travel. *Transport Reviews* 33(3):255–270.

D. Metz. 2013b. Mobility, access and choice: a new source of evidence. *Journal of Transport and Land Use* 6(2):1–4.

D. Metz. 2014. *Peak Car: The Future of Travel*. London: Landor LINKS.

D. Metz. 2015a. Peak car in the big city: reducing London's greenhouse gas emissions. *Case Studies on Transport Policy* 3(4):367–371.

D. Metz. 2015b. Future of cities: beyond 'peak car'. Government Office for Science, London.

D. Metz. 2016. Changing demographics. In *Handbook on Transport and Urban Planning in the Developed World*, edited by M. Bliemer, C. Mulley and C. Moutou. Cheltenham: Edward Elgar.

POST. 2013. Peak car use in Britain. Parliamentary Office of Science and Technology, London.

E. Quinet and R. Vickerman. 2004. *Principles of Transport Economics*. Cheltenham: Edward Elgar.

L. Raikes. 2016. Connecting lines: how devolving transport policy can transform our cities. Institute for Public Policy Research North, Manchester.

D. Rodrik. 2015. *Economics Rules*. New York: W. W. Norton.

B. Rosewell. 2010. Planning curses: how to deliver long term investment in infrastructure. Policy Exchange, London.

Social Research Associates. 2015. On the move: exploring attitudes to road and rail travel in Britain. Independent Transport Commission, London.

T. Venables, J. Laird and H. Overman. 2014. Transport investment and economic performance: implications for project appraisal. Department for Transport, London.

S. Verma. 2014. Customer technology: the ticket to greater mobility. In *Moving Cities: The Future of Urban Travel*, edited by S. Glaister and E. Box. London: RAC Foundation.

C. Wolmar. 2014. What's the point of HS2? *London Review of Books* 36(8):3–7.

C. Wolmar. 2016. *Are Trams Socialist? Why Britain Has No Transport Policy.* London Publishing Partnership.

T. Worsley. 2011. The evolution of London's Crossrail scheme and the development of the Department for Transport's economic appraisal methods. Discussion Paper 2011-27, International Transport Forum, OECD, Paris.

T. Worsley and P. Mackie. 2015. Transport policy, appraisal and decision-making. RAC Foundation, London.

Jim O'Neill's *The BRIC Road to Growth* (published 2013) calls for an urgent overhaul of global economic governance to reflect the reality of the economic power of the BRIC countries and others, especially Korea. Even though their growth rates will slow compared with recent decades, they are key players in the global economy. Jim argues that while the BRIC countries all have stabilizing adjustments to make, there is much for the developed nations in the West to learn from them.

ISBN: 978-1-907994-13-5

Bridget Rosewell's *Reinventing London* (published 2013) tells the story of a city that has enjoyed an extraordinary period of growth in the past generation, symbolized by the towers of Canary Wharf built on the skeleton of the old docks. Finance was at the heart of this, so how can London's economy be reinvented after the financial crisis? An early decision on airport investment to improve global links is a must, given that the capital's main airport is full to capacity.

ISBN: 978-1-907994-14-2

Andrew Sentance's *Rediscovering Growth: After the Crisis* (published 2013) discusses the difficult economic climate in Europe and the US and predicts that it is set to continue for many years, despite desperate efforts to stimulate growth. The long phase of expansion in Western economies that lasted from the 1980s until 2008 was driven by easy money, cheap imports and confidence – all gone.

ISBN: 978-1-907994-15-9

Julia Unwin's *Why Fight Poverty?* (published 2013) looks back at the struggle to end poverty and asks if it has been worth it. What would a poverty-free country be like? Julia concludes that we urgently need to resolve poverty, because it is costly, wasteful and risky, but that we can only create a strong, shared understanding of poverty and how to end it when we recognize that 'they' are people like 'us'.

ISBN: 978-1-907994-16-6

David Birch's *Identity Is The New Money* (published 2014) argues that identity is changing profoundly and that money is changing equally profoundly. Because of technological change the two trends are converging so that all that we need for transacting will be our identities captured in the unique record of our online social contacts. Social networks and mobile phones are the key technologies.

ISBN: 978-1-907994-12-8

Kate Barker's *Housing: Where's the Plan?* (published 2014) argues that home ownership is out of reach of a growing number of people. Government finds it easier to introduce short-term policies that are not really effective, meaning that the long-term issues are never really resolved. Reforms are urgently needed. This book dispels some common myths, and provides answers in the form of policy recommendations.

ISBN: 978-1-907994-11-1

David Fell's *Bad Habits, Hard Choices: Using the Tax System to Make Us Healthier* (published 2016) argues that the curious mix of taxes and duties the British face are messy, opaque, out of date – and unfair, with more of your income going to pay these taxes the poorer you are. Drawing on insights from behavioural economics, David concludes that there is a fair, inclusive, adaptable, affordable and resilient way of enabling us to eat healthily and to tackle the obesity crisis.

ISBN: 978-1-907994-50-0

Danny Dorling's *A Better Politics: How Government Can Make Us Happier* (published spring 2016) aims to inspire a politics that will enable future generations to be happier, with greater well-being and better health being the goals rather than wealth maximization. The evidence for a successful politics that would promote happiness and health is examined, and policies that take account of this evidence are suggested.

ISBN: 978-1-907994-53-1

Christian Wolmar's *Are Trams Socialist?* (published spring 2016) is an entertaining polemic that argues that it is not too far fetched to say that there has never been a transport policy in the UK – and one is clearly needed. The book suggests elements that such a policy could include, drawing on successful examples that can be seen elsewhere in Europe, and argues that courage and clear thinking are needed if these ideas are to be implemented.

ISBN: 978-1-907994-56-2

David Metz's *Travel Fast or Smart? A Manifesto for an Intelligent Transport Policy* (published autumn 2016) sets out the principles that could underpin a strategic policy for transport. The book argues that we need to think about how and where we want the economy to develop – and about how new digital technologies can help us achieve what is needed – instead of focusing piecemeal on getting from place to place ever faster.

ISBN: 978-1-907994-59-3

All titles in the **Perspectives** series are available to buy from London Publishing Partnership's website with free UK postage and packing:

http://londonpublishingpartnership.co.uk/perspectives-series/